Writers Praise
Put Off My Sackcloth

There aren't many people who change the trajectory of their relationship to their world. The depressed usually remain depressed. The complainers. . . complain. The pleasers, keep pleasing. The contexts change as they encounter different life stages. But their outlook remains the same from childhood to death.

Annie Dawid's essays in *Put Off My Sackcloth*, aren't for the faint-hearted. She shines light on the slippery slope of mental health, the brutality of humans past and present. We are shepherded into the pivotal moments that lead to a good life or one that can't be salvaged. Her grappling with these difficulties head-on, her perseverance in seeing and knowing, her quest for a broader view infused with love, bring us to a new posture. She shows us the light that comes through the cracks, if we are brave enough to see it.

Sarah Michaelson, producer of *The Voice Box*, a documentary of healing

Annie Dawid's essays slow dance with her idea for a novel. After reading "All Thy Waves," the opening essay which is troubling in its honesty about depression and suicide, one wants to hold this writer dear, keep her close. Dawid cannot forget November 18, 1978. On that day the world stopped before succumbing to shock over the suicide of 918 people. Can a novel ever explain Jim Jones and Jonestown? Dawid wants to write one. What happened to the people of Peoples Temple? From her landscape of mountains in Colorado, Dawid gathers the fragments of her own life creating essays, humble in their tone, but struggling to breathe, to understand the identity which links her to Jewish ancestors who saw their own paradise lost. What demons must we survive? Why is death's kiss too often sweet? When the coyotes sing at night, how do we answer the howl that calls for us to take our lives? For many years Annie Dawid has been listening, writing.

E. Ethelbert Miller, writer and literary activist, host of *On The Margin* (WPFW 89.3 FM)

D0880505

Dawid's *Put Off My Sackcloth* is both lyrically reflective, and crisp in its journalistic exposition. In spite of the tenderness and yearnings throughout this collection of essays, one reads within a history of killing: mass killings, single shootings, private soul killings. Yet, Dawid engages over and over with the poetry of philosophy and memory, and precisely paints each of the characters, who range from the landscape itself to the travelers journeying the geography of the soul.

Elizabeth Burns, author of *Tilt*

These essays bear witness to a life lived with emotional courage and intellectual integrity. Through dark and harrowing years of personal struggle, and her parallel inquiry into the psychology of Jonestown, the solaces of community, motherhood, and her beloved landscape in rural southern Colorado weave their bright threads.

Carol Guerrero-Murphy, author, *Chained Dog Dreams* and *Bright Path Dark River*, Professor *Emerita* Prison College Program

If you are an artist hounded by a calling you can't escape, this book is for you. If you were born broken-hearted, this book is for you. If you think you know nothing or something about race or guns or poetry or dance or love or suicide or porcupines or politics, you have in your hands, the book you've been waiting for.

Reginald McKnight, author, *He Sleeps* and *White Boys*

Part memoir, part essay collection, part author's journal, *Put Off My Sackcloth* is completely fascinating. Annie Dawid's reflections on her own life, and on the lives of others, capture the times we live in with honesty and insight. In particular, her efforts to retell the story of Jonestown in a new way offer fresh insights into the infamous mass murders/suicides of 1978. But the book is larger than a single event, and the remarkable essays and reflections in *Put Off My Sackcloth* stick with you long after you put the book down.

Rebecca Moore, Ph.D.

Reading Annie Dawid's essays for the first time, the question in my mind is: How have I lived so long in this world without reading Annie Dawid's essays? In *Put Off My Sackcloth*, there are accidents and suicide attempts, drugs and accidents, guns and broken bodies—but Dawid's intelligence and humor light up the darkest landscapes. In these essays, Dawid never flinches and when she can laugh, she laughs. She takes us down deep, but she shows us the sparkle of light glinting at the exit of the cave—and love? Love wins.

Jill Christman, author of *Darkroom: A Family Exposure* and *Borrowed Babies*

For Lisa,
dear neighbor
and now
winter-friend,
with affection,
Annie
in Monument 11/6/21

Put Off My Sackcloth:

Essays

[signature]

Annie Dawid
2021

The Humble Essayist
Press

The Humble Essayist Press
Blairsville, Georgia

for Isaiah,

my best beloved

INTRODUCTION
by Kathryn Winograd

In Annie Dawid's essay, "Babysitter Goes to War," the eighteen-year-old in glittering braces, who cares for Dawid's young son, pronounces that he will go to Iraq to prove that he has "what it takes to be a man."

"How will you be of use to the world as another casualty?" Dawid asks him.

It is this simple question that Dawid confronts throughout this collection of essays, whether that casualty be a babysitter, a stranger, a loved one or Dawid faltering in the 20th century maelstrom of war and drugs and depression and modern-day massacre that can and does annihilate the very youngest of our school children. Into this mosaic of memory Dawid takes us, holding out for us yet another chip of painted light to finger under the estranged sun.

Like the question, this collection could be a simple journey: once there was a sad girl from a sad family with a sad life. And one night she stood on a twelfth-floor balcony, holding her child in her arms.

But there is nothing simple here in this essay collection crafted by a writer, scholar, professor, journalist, daughter of a holocaust survivor, a modern woman who finds in the reckonings of T.S. Eliot's "Wasteland" her own fragments that she will gather against her ruins, "harvesting bits of self," as she describes it, "scattered like meteorites everywhere."

The world Dawid lives in is fractured, a world of terrible raw beauty and terrible raw woundings. The unexpected ground of her own beseeching, of her own search for a faith she never thought to want, is the valley beneath the Sangre de Cristo mountains, Blood of Christ, named by a Spanish explorer in the red-light of an evening, a solitary place of cattle and wandering coyote and abandoned troughs she seeds with wildflowers. These essays on this place serve as touchstones, a mounting collection of light against the interior darkness that has haunted Dawid for half a century, Dawid drawing from this sanctity the power to examine a painful past of which she once said how endlessly we forget and how endlessly we repeat.

"What I pursue is clarity," Dawid tells us.

The author and essayist, Robert Root, in his essay, "Collage, Montage, Mosaic, Vignette, Episode, Segment," suggests that "the more complex the story is, the more interwoven with other subjects, ideas, incidents, experiences, the harder it is to make it all connect in a linear way." The difficulties lie in how "the connections and associations that come so readily in the memory and in the imagination often deny simple linearity, easy transition from one subtopic to the next." These essays are written across and around time, moving between past and present, moving between "hanging trees" and sackcloth, woodfire stoves and "sky gods" of Jonestown, pizza and pirouettes, Camus and Beloveds, debilitating depression and self-annihilation and moments of found joy.

Not the singular essay but the whole collective becomes the mosaic. What does creative nonfiction allow us to do but journey into the mind and the heart of our past, its shadows and light, its gaps and recursiveness, to find pattern and meaning in what we thought once was isolated, coincidental? Dawid tells us about *les invisibles*, in Haiti, "the spirits of the dead who are with us, always, whether we honor them or not." Dawid keeps going back into the stories of her past, the people she knew living or dead now, and herself as a girl, a young woman, the middle-aged mother-to-be, these selves of her past her own *invisibles*. She can say, here, I stood on this balcony with my child and thought to jump, and, here, I listened to the words of a man who thought himself god and so nine hundred poisoned themselves for him and, here, I rode my bike on a dark dark night and broke my teeth, and, here, a married man put his arms around my waist when I was young and made pizza and I wanted him, and, here, a man for six days lived against the crush of a decomposing friend, and, here, I pumped my milk in a psych ward, and, here, and everywhere, I loved my son.

Dawid leads us through this collection of essays by juxtaposition, allusion, parallelism, nuance, and heart. Dawid's career as a writer has foremost been as a fiction writer, beginning with her first book, *York Ferry*, first reviewed by the *New York Times*, and her latest book, *Paradise Undone: A Novel of Jonestown*, sections of which continue to pick up prizes as Dawid searches for a home for it. But she is also a poet, a journalist, a playwright. Yet, for me, all of Dawid's talents and craft have always spiraled together in her nonfiction: her brilliant scholarship and analysis, the largess of her consciousness and empathy, her searing, unflinching honesty and keen eye for detail, the precision and lyricism of her prose, the sophistication of her ability to "tell a yarn."

I think back to Dawid's question to that earnest babysitter burying himself already in a war of which he understands little. Of what use would Dawid be to this world if she were a casualty? In reading the mysteries of her father's will, Dawid one day finds her father's clear message from the grave:

"Beloved, you are still young. Make another life."

And so she does. And for that we are lucky.

Kathryn Winograd is an editor for The Humble Essayist Press and the author of *Phantom Canyon: Essays of Reclamation* and *Slow Arrow: Unearthing the Frail Children*

I have set before you life and death,
blessing and cursing:
Therefore choose life,
that both thou and thy seed may live

Deuteronomy 30:19

TABLE OF CONTENTS

PUBLICATIONS FROM THE COLLECTION

"All Thy Waves," winner 2012 Dana Award in the Essay;
shorter version, "Deeps," winner 2013 Northern Colorado Non-Fiction Award,
anthologized in *Pooled Ink*, 2014
"Almost," *BioStories* 2016
"Arrival," *Colorado Central* 2010
"Babysitter Goes to War," *Pilgrimage* 2008
The Beloved Essays:
"Introducing My Beloved to this Part of the World," *Cañon Beat* 2011
Needle-in-the-Hay 2016
"The Thinking Cabin," *Cañon Beat* 2011; *We Said Go Travel* 2016
"Creature Visitations," *Cañon Beat* 2011
"Cabin-bound at 9100 feet," *Cañon Beat* 2011;
anthologized in *The Beautifullest* 2020
"Dome Life," online & audio, *The Drum* 2013
"Espresso Induces," *Spelk*, September 30, 2015
"Extratemporal," *Progenitor* 2014; *Echapbook: Rites of Passage* 2018
"Fathom These Events: A Writer's Journal," *Jonestown Report* 2005
"Four Protagonists, One Author," *Jonestown Report* 2007
"The Fox Breaks the Code," winner, short-short,
online, *Literal Latté* 2008;
anthologized in *Flash in the Attic 2*, 2016
"How Came These Things to Pass?" anthologized in
Humans in the Wild: Reactions to a Gun-Loving Country 2020
"Les Invisibles at the Dinner Table," *Cañon Beat* 2009;
Fig Tree Books Newsletter Jan. 2020
"Jonestown, a 'Hard Sell'" *Jonestown Report* 2009
"A Long and Suffering People," *Jonestown Report* 2013
"Metaphor, b. 1978," *Jonestown Report* 2010
"Nitza Kosher Pizza," *Los Angeles Review* Spring 2013
"Queen of the Dogs," *Cañon Beat* 2011
"Rescued and Humble," *Cañon Beat* 2010

"Sacred and Profane Dances," *Progenitor* 2013;
London Independent Story Project 2020
"Saying Farewell to Jonestown," *Jonestown Report* 2010
"Teeth," *Common Ground* 2011
"Welcome, Now Leave," *Denver Post* 2007
"What They Call Him," *Windmill* 2018; anthologized in
*Excavating Honesty: An Anthology of Rage
and Hope in America,* 2016
"What They Chose," *Jonestown Report* 2006
"A Writer's Journal, Part II," *Jonestown Report* 2006
"The Yuck Factor," *Jonestown Report* 2007

ALL THY WAVES
1999

For my soul is full of troubles: and my life draweth nigh unto the grave.
I am counted with them that go down into the pit:
I am as a man that hath no
strength.

Thou hast laid me in the lowest pit, in darkness, in the deeps.
Thy wrath lieth hard upon me, and thou hast afflicted me
with all thy waves.

from Psalm 88

During my last sojourn in That Place, I could listen only to Marian Anderson and Paul Robeson singing mournful, soothing gospel. I could read only literature from the nineteenth century and earlier. In the solipsism of my condition, I discovered that King David's Psalms described depression with beauty and accuracy, and I found some solace there. I ate only cereal, and that with effort. I could not bear the sun and prayed for rain. Nights were marginally better, when I did not have to confront the light. In the wooded park where I walked my dogs, I found the darkest places and the least-trod paths. On one bend of a trail I'd never seen before, I discovered the hanging tree. Like a car wreck, it drew me back again and again. I didn't want to study it, to want what it promised, but I was defenseless against its allure. Every afternoon I walked around the old oak, admiring its solid, sturdy arm under which I believed I would achieve my final rest, like a bird, nesting. As school was out, I did not teach and had no daily obligations. I was six months' pregnant – six months off my meds.

Friends worried, though I only hinted at the nature of That Place, where I was once again residing, a familiar neighborhood to me during a lifetime lasting – hard for me to believe – thirty-nine years so far, though I felt sure I couldn't breathe that toxic air much longer. Six months earlier, ecstatic, the proverbial

1

biological clock inside my body suddenly wound and humming after years of desire, I thanked all the powers, gods and spirits as I read the results of my blood test. A hitherto unknown sensation of peace flooded through me as I walked alone across the OB/GYN waiting room in which, with my gray hair, I appeared twenty years older than all the other women, expectantly awaiting news alongside husbands, boyfriends and mothers.

Despite a decade of therapy and medication, depression inevitably followed elation, as pride goeth ineluctably before a fall, but my brand-new condition seemed somehow outside the parameters of that lifelong template. Proverbially, I glowed. Never once experiencing morning sickness, I gloated, considering myself of stronger stuff than a friend who puked every morning for the first three months. Wanting a healthy, natural child, I stopped taking anything that might harm Helen/Elijah ~ ~ I chose to be surprised by my child's sex ~ including alcohol, tobacco, aspirin, refined sugar and anti-depressants.

Only many months later did I recall a psychopharmacologist, whom I'd once consulted when it seemed my ordinary medications (Prozac and Trazodone) and excellent therapist were not helping me extend my stays long enough outside That Place. After testing me, the doctor decided I'd been misdiagnosed and really my problem was Obsessive-Compulsive Disorder, which often masqueraded as depression. Obsessive thought and behavior described my siblings and me perfectly; Dr. H. had healed me with a new diagnosis, or so I wanted to believe. He prescribed Luvox, and for a while all was rosy, with my spanking new label and a medication that sounded like love. Should I ever become pregnant, he insisted, I would need to return for help in getting through pregnancy, as Luvox would not be appropriate. Perhaps I filed that information in the need-to-know folder I imagined I kept at the ready in the back of my brain, beside other memories I deemed not especially useful. Or perhaps, even then, I thought I knew better; pregnancy itself, I presumed, would be the medicine for what ailed me, and medication superfluous.

Initially, it was. Pregnant, I felt gleeful and generous. Knowing my reputation for tough, no-nonsense instruction, my students were perhaps surprised to confront this jolly, roly-poly silver-haired professor quite unlike the unflappable, take-no-bullshit teacher of college lore. As I didn't disclose my pregnancy until safely past the common miscarriage timeline, and the results of my amniocentesis were in without initiating a struggle over keeping or aborting a child with Downs Syndrome, students and colleagues alike must have assumed a change in my spirit that came with approaching 40.

"Lighten up," was advice I'd heard all my life and always found banal, inappropriate to a world smeared in suffering, a darkness I assumed veiled the lives of most human beings, for how could it not?

In the summer of 1999, abruptly battened inside That Place, I blamed the Columbine Massacre for such rude transport, its fusillade of child-inspired violence restoring the veil, obscuring the light I had come to trust, foolishly, as my new abode. The Colorado high school, which I'd driven past many times, was a few minutes from an old friend's home; her daughters would attend that school some day. As immediate as if it were the school down the block from me, to which my child would one day go, Columbine's particular horror re-emphasized ~ because I had indeed forgotten ~ true nature of existence. What had I been thinking to bring a child into a world of Columbines? Ever a news junkie, I devoured the papers and kept the radio on all day, suffusing myself in terror. For the first time, added to familiar depression was a previously unknown anxiety; I felt anxious every wakeful minute. Hoping for a simple solution, I eliminated all caffeine; I took baths and sipped Calming Tea, but with prodigious time to fill, no longer able to concentrate on the small print of *David Copperfield* or *New Grub Street*, I worried.

I worried about everything I had not worried about before: I couldn't afford a child, I thought. I couldn't provide the support Helen/Elijah would need from a single parent. Most importantly and obviously, I didn't have the mental stamina to be a parent, just as I had always believed to be true about myself until the biological clock startled me with its alarm at 36, muffling previous fears and good sense.

In the most painful part of that turning from joy to sorrow, a close friend made it known she thought I would fail to be a good mother, due to my proclivity toward depression, from which she also suffered. Before the turning, I scoffed at her words, hurt but in no way destroyed. I read her many-paged, handwritten letter on legal yellow paper as I walked jauntily up a path in Forest Park across town, in the days when I felt powerful and free, walking my two mutts with my big belly and no worries. I threw the letter away; what was the purpose of it? Did she believe her words would prompt me toward a late-term abortion because she thought I was incapable of mothering? I laughed at how wrong she was, how limited in her imagination.

After the turning, I could only agree: she knew me better than I knew myself, I thought. She knew the true me, the me who was at core a depressed and hopeless self, certainly not mother material. To help me from the pit, she called all my other friends to set up an Annie-watch, to make sure I was surviving, but the other friends detected *schadenfreude* and kept their distance from her. Later, I felt it too, when I regained an awareness of the world beyond despair. Many years passed before we were able to repair that breach of trust.

With time and perspective, I realized Columbine was merely a bad coincidence, and the less dramatic, chemical truth was that every time I'd quit my medication in the past decade ~ and who hasn't, feeling so much better and believing drugs wicked, for the morally weak ~ six months later, with a criminal calendrical efficiency, I would descend into the suicidally friendly darkness of That Place in a kind of homecoming. I found peculiar comfort there. It was, after all, familiar, *gemütlich*, reminding me of my childhood home, unlike the land of light, to which I was a relative stranger. At the time, Columbine and the hormones of pregnancy seemed stronger than the inexorable pull of blood, but now I see it was after all exactly like the fall of 1996, not pregnant and unprompted by any Columbines, when I walked a path outside a writers' retreat in Scotland, searching for the proper cliff from which to throw myself into a gorge. For the six months prior to that dark October, I'd experienced bliss, free of medication's stigma, writing fiction furiously, in love with Colorado light and the in-cloud lightning of summer storms.

And that episode was just like 1993, again abroad, when I found myself at Lands End, six months' gone from Prozac, in St. Ives, Cornwall, where I could glimpse Virginia Woolf's lighthouse whenever the fog failed to blot it from the horizon. In the cold rain and despair I succumbed to my truth that, unlike other people, I was not meant for this life. The ends of the earth drew me for a reason, for my own end. "There are other places which also are the world's end," writes T.S. Eliot in "Little Gidding." "Some at the sea jaws, or over a dark lake, but this is the nearest, in place and time, now and in England." Like King David, Thomas Stearns Eliot knew depression like a mother, I am sure of it.

What saved me from the hanging tree, the river gorge outside Edinburgh, and the Atlantic off the Cornish Coast were, I believed at the time, piddling details. In the first case, I worried what would happen to my dogs. And, more importantly, what if some child found me bulbous-eyed, hanging on a red dog leash as she raced along the path, thrilled to be flying on her new two-wheeler? No. I would never involve a stranger ~ especially a child ~ in my demise. In Scotland, I wondered what would happen to my body, fearing to involve my parents with an overseas casket-transport, and in the last case, in the relentless rain near Woolf's summer home, I discovered that the waistband of my silk trousers had lost its elastic, and during my walk, unbeknownst to me, the gold harem pants had descended to my knees, blaring my long underwear to the world. Of course, no one else was walking in the downpour that afternoon at Lands End, so my shame was all my own. Only later could I see the humor in it, the slapstick quality of a suicidal woman diverted from the deed by her golden fancy pants' dysfunction, but at the time it was a terrible humiliation from which I had to flee. Returned to my room at the bed & breakfast, which was cold and unwelcoming, I went on living.

Not "mere" details but a proclivity toward life, the biological drive to live ~ not die ~ kept me going. "Urge, urge, urge, always the procreant urge of the world," wrote Whitman, who did not procreate in the traditional sense but pressed every moment toward living.

In my pre-medicated years, in the early 1980s, not six months past the serotonin deadline but an entire lifetime, I roamed another Lands End at the western edge of San Francisco, thinking the same despairing thoughts, wanting to die. The Pacific Ocean would be a wistful name for my unmarked grave. In those days I discovered a temporary solace in alcohol. In therapy but before the days of minimal side-effect anti-depressants, I abhorred the notion of drugs, remembering my mother on Valium, tranquilized into nothingness. Better depressed than empty, I concluded, better suicidal than a zombie.

When I was 12, my mother tried to kill herself, and every moment after that middle-of-the-night, dreamlike event darkened my life with despair, ordinary problems twisted by the possibility of a suicidal solution. Only in my early twenties with a good therapist did I begin to understand this distortion of my adolescence, the way I had shouldered my mother's depression in the futile hope of saving her, to prove my love and loyalty. But understanding did not enlighten me. To the contrary, I found such new awareness more frightening than my vague, pre-analysis unknowingness, so I drank to keep it at bay.

During my early-to-mid twenties, my grad school friend Victoria and I visited bars together and drank until we could hardly see, often winding up in strangers' beds, behaving in what was to us unconsciously but to anyone else obviously suicidal behavior. Four o'clock in the morning with a group of guys in a car next to a park in the heart of the city ~ what exactly did we think would happen?

At 39, however, I believed myself beyond such delusional thinking and self-destructive acts. Hadn't I spent many years and thousands of dollars on the psychiatrist's couch? Hadn't I pushed beyond my puritanical view of medication's disrepute and tried most every pharmaceutical manufactured to mend me? Wasn't I completely in charge of a life that appeared to outsiders accomplished and full? And finally, wasn't I fantastically lucky to get pregnant so easily at such a late date when many women of my age were struggling to do so? No longer the caricature of an unhappy post-adolescent roaming the San Francisco hills at night, an A-student binge drinking on weekends and sleeping with men whose names I didn't want to remember, I was a professor, published and sober. Not only did I see myself as too sophisticated for a black-and-white worldview, but it was unworthy and selfish of a woman in the upper middle-class tax bracket to imagine she was suffering. So much of the world lived in misery; I had no right to my despair.

The most helpful thing a doctor ever told me was the following: on scans of severely depressed people, whole sections of their brains remained unilluminated, completely out of service.

In the dusk of my suicidal depression and the seventh month of my pregnancy, after trying to hang myself with the red dog leash ~ too short ~ on a rafter in the basement ~ too flimsy for my bulk ~ I ended up on the Kaiser psychiatrist's couch. My OB/GYN nurse practitioner had sent me there after requiring weekly visits to her office, simply to make me appear for appointments, and witnessing, at the start of my last trimester, a sudden failure to thrive. Instead of gaining, I lost weight, and, despite the apparent health of my fetus, I was inquiring about how to "adopt out" the child who would shortly be born to me. After the inadequate rafter experience, and an afternoon with a purposely broken glass in the bathtub, I concluded that I needed to kill myself *after* the birth. For an adult of sound mind ~ which I believed myself to possess ~ to commit suicide was a right in a world in which one had control of one's destiny ~ a privilege on a planet where most had no such agency. But to murder another ~ akin to including the hypothetical bike-riding girl in the park ~ was unconscionable. After all, I did have standards. So I decided to live ~ for a while, at any rate, until my due date of September 1st ~ and to see the doctor who, according to my nurse practitioner, had lots of experience with depressed pregnant women. Having only heard of *post*-partum depression, I considered myself an anomaly, typically, depressed at the wrong time, an asshole to be wanting to die while a friend my age in another city had been trying for years to conceive and failing.

Why did the doctor's description of a depressed brain's malfunction perforate my darkness? Despite all my reading, education, and therapy, there remained inside me enough of my German father's stoicism to deplore my condition as symptomatic of weakness, an indicator of a feeble will. After all, my father had escaped the Nazis and hadn't succumbed to depression. He'd lost his mother at 12, most of his family had been exterminated in his twenties, his first grandchild had died of an obscure, genetic Jewish disease, and he'd had to commit his wife and son to psychiatric wards more than once, but he'd never been depressed, or so I told myself. What was my failing, if not weakness? As the smart daughter, the accomplished child most like my father, I could not admit, much less demonstrate to the world, likeness to my pathetic, crazy mother.

Whole sections of my brain, said Doctor O, were either operating at sub-par levels or not functioning at all. Like the outer world, the inside of my brain had slowed itself to crawl in darkness. Studies had proved that the eyes of severely depressed people could not recognize all the colors in the spectrum, he told me. It was as if the patient had suffered a head injury in a motorcycle accident, or fallen from a height onto concrete. This scientific fact, something empirical that even my steely, brilliant father could not deny, managed to penetrate the veil of my despair. To my mind, his likening of a mental state to a physical one reduced the stigma, making my condition seem less a question of will than of cerebral chemistry. Certain medications, Doctor O insisted, could help me while not harming Helen/Elijah. Because my due date was so close, and I knew babies could be born at 7 or 8 months without long-term, life-damaging results, I decided to accept his counsel. If I could live long enough to deliver the baby safely, to hand him or her over to a loving stranger, then it would be enough. I started on a low dose of Paxil, which he hoped would diminish my anxiety as well.

A few days later, my pregnant self, my father and brother were drifting down the Willamette River on a faux steamboat, the recorded info-spiel too loud in our ears. In the group of tourists by the bar stood a very pregnant young blonde, drinking beer and smoking a cigarette with what looked like extended family and partner/husband. People stared, but no one said anything. What an irresponsible mother, everyone was surely thinking. Completely unselfconscious, she seemed to be having a wonderful time, chatting and laughing. I marveled at her brazen flaunting of the unwritten law that now prohibits all smoking and drinking for pregnant women ~ at least in public. Watching the populated riverbanks diminish as we floated south, barely able to speak as depression still compressed me, I asked myself how could I condemn her nicotine and alcohol infusions when I had come so close to destroying my child in a far more drastic way?

My father had flown out from New York, and my brother up from California to check on me. When they'd made the reservations months before, I'd anticipated an interesting parental/filial/sibling relation "learning lab" ~ my old therapist's phrase for family visits ~ but nothing dire. After the turning, I pleaded with them not to come, but my sudden resistance-without-a-reason affirmed their resolve to see me.

Each day of the new med regime and a life of regular appointments scheduled with Doctor O, I struggled to feel a millimeter better, to detect one iota of improvement inside me. Did the light hurt a bit less today? Did I feel a trifle less unhinged as I managed to eat a meal out with Steve and Baba, my close, quasi-parental friends? At the diner I managed a milkshake, and afterward, window-shopping on the way to Ben & Jerry's for Baba's lemon sherbet, I ducked into an upscale hardware store's entryway and began to cry. Steve had been telling a story and stopped, mid-sidewalk, to find me gone. In the alcove, when I told them I wanted to give my baby away, they didn't raise their voices in shock, or tell me I was absurd. "You're feeling that bad, huh," Steve said, rubbing my back as I wiped my eyes, leaning incongruously against the display of fancy gardening tools speckled with packages of heirloom tomato seeds.

"Oh honey," said Baba, hugging me, "it's not going to be like this always."

I trusted them; they had raised children and helped with grandchildren, had their own extensive histories with depression and anxiety. It was Baba who had recommended the renowned psychopharmacologist Dr. H to me years back, after he'd helped alter her days from troubled to tolerable to terrific. In her fifties, she said, she was finally enjoying daily life. Steve was one of many colleagues with whom I could talk anti-depressant dosages along with how to teach Modernism ~ a number of us English professor-types knew similar darkness.

My father was staying at the Hilton downtown, my brother with me, and in my little Honda I was driving us all over town, with or without the two dogs' accompaniment. The two male members of my family of origin tended to argue often. Although we were all now old, gray, balding or bald, it seemed to me the discourse hadn't changed much between my brother and father from the days of the younger screaming "Fuck you!" at the dining room table, blaming my father for all his ills.

At 20, my brother had descended into another genre of pit, diagnosed first as schizophrenic, then manic-depressive. Was his version of the family pathology more typically male? Instead of self-destructing in the female fashion, he struck out, testosterone fueling a brief stay in jail after punching a Mercedes Benz that nearly hit his dog; another time, he drove a car onto our lawn and yelled expletives at all of us ~ I was a "little rich bitch" ~ then wrenched the screen door from its hinges. My parents called the police. After running away from various psych wards, the chi-chi private ones as well as bare-bones state ones, he ended up sojourning in his bedroom for many months, eating cereal and watching television, a zombie on Thorazine. I never knew who he was, nor did I try, as his certifiably crazy behavior terrified me. First Mom, now big brother ~ surely, I would be next if I didn't take considerable care. My big sister had apparently escaped the morass by marrying young and exiting the family manse. One day, my brother left for California, poised by the highway with his thumb pointing west, and never returned.

Nevertheless, a couple of decades hadn't much diminished the tension, my father seeing my brother as a now middle-aged failure and my brother still charging my octogenarian father with his own shortcomings. Nowadays, however, we were more polite and did not use epithets. My position as the fucked up kid was novel for everyone ~ in its nakedness, at any rate ~ and such strangeness elicited their generosity, sublimating their age-old battle, at least temporarily. At dinner, my brother very sensibly deconstructed my list of distresses. My father reassured me not to worry about money. Neither understood how my former thrilled optimism about impending motherhood had metamorphosed into its opposite of constant dread. Over salmon at a chic restaurant downtown, they tried to talk me into hopefulness. I didn't disclose the particulars of my recent descent into the pit, but I did admit to suffering from depression in the past, and intimated that it was again upon me like a curse.

"See a doctor!" my father commanded in his brusque, Berliner way.

"I have," I told him.

"Good."

In my twenties and thirties, when I'd asked him to pay, he'd resented my seeing shrinks, as though his youngest child's regular trips to the psychiatrist condemned him somehow. His wife and son had resided in crazy wards, while I had, to all appearances, avoided them, climbing the white-collar ladder to higher and higher education until, like him, I had a doctor degree. My sister became a secretary and stay-home mom like my mother, and my brother lived in his van, working when he worked at all for a delivery service. I was the professor, the one who liked to travel, who published books and could speak other languages. Together, we had visited Brussels, Telluride, Taxco and St. Petersburg.

So what on earth did I need to see a psychiatrist for? "Freud ruined civilization," my father liked to say. Freud wasn't the only culprit, however. Perhaps it was being born into privilege that had harmed us, our lack of struggle. Not only did we have every financial opportunity for advancement, but we were white American citizens, growing up unafraid of persecution, tyranny, and impending war at home. During the World War I embargo of German ports, my father's teeth turned brown from scurvy. His mother died of pernicious anemia when he was still a child, and his father had struggled to make a living during the Weimar Republic, and lost his job in Hitler's 1935 decree. They survived as well as they could, relying on the income of the Gentile stepmother librarian.

In response to these troubles, my father did not crumple, did not self-destruct with anxiety and/or depression. Instead, he worked harder. With a shrewd finesse of the rules, he managed to continue studying law despite the edict prohibiting Jews from doing so. In 1936, he wrote a book on the expanding number of anti-Semitic laws in Germany and found a publisher for it. In 1939, he finagled his way onto the last boat out of Genoa, bound for Shanghai. Under threat to his very life, he thrived.

Like the children of many such refugees to the United States, his offspring had known nothing of comparable struggle. My teeth were orthodontically straightened and healthy ~ at least until I fell on my face at 25 in an earlier suicidal moment, that time by a dark lake, drunk on a bicycle alone in the night, leading to a trip to the emergency room and years at the prosthodontist. But in the U.S., no one in government or business demanded our jobs, our homes, or our lives because we were Jewish. My father never blamed us for these circumstances, but I couldn't help my guilt at failing to thrive, though I'd spent a lifetime covering up these failures. Succeeding, for the most part, until now.

After their departure, for reasons I couldn't quite pinpoint, I felt slightly better. At the end of July, my birthing classes scheduled for the following weekend, I began to read in preparation for what I was determined would be an entirely natural, drug-free birth. Although I still felt strange everywhere I went, a depressed alien in the land of happy Portlanders, happy because it was summer and therefore sunny while I worked hard to avoid the light and couldn't remember how to smile, the impending end of pregnancy encouraged me. While I was no longer 100% sure of my adoption-then-suicide plan, I remained in a holding pattern, reserving judgment.

On Friday, Baba and I went shopping for a bassinette, the last big purchase I had yet to make. (Evidently, I didn't foresee giving up the baby until after I had made use of the ideal, sheltering bassinette.) It was hot, my car had no air-conditioning, and we stopped for something cold before heading to the baked flatlands of the outer avenues where Babies R Us had its outlet. Sitting in the drive-through lane at Burgerville, U.S.A., I discovered one could get shots of espresso in a mocha milkshake. A former coffee junkie, I'd been without caffeine for months, and I still don't know what possessed me to ask for a double, but I did.

In short order, I began to feel better, more like the self I remembered. In the back of a horrid warehouse-like emporium, I found The Bassinette ~ unpainted wicker and Victorian, with wheels to move it from room to room. The cushion and pillow were soft white cotton, trimmed with eyelets, and I could envision my baby inside it, protected and peaceful. The price was more than I'd wanted to spend, but I bought it anyway, encouraged by Baba to trust my instinct ~ a certainty I hadn't felt in forever. It wouldn't fit in the Honda, so Steve promised to pick it up in his truck the next day. All afternoon I yakked and even laughed ~ the caffeine had powered me back into life, or so it felt. In the morning was my first birthing class, and I was looking forward to it.

That night, I couldn't sleep. I mean I never fell asleep, reading *The Birth Partner*, feeling so alive I couldn't shut my eyes. Though I blamed the caffeine for my inability to rest, I was simultaneously grateful, as that double-espresso mocha milkshake appeared to have re-set my clock, springing me back into the land of the living.

When Brooke picked me up at 8:30 a.m. for the class, weird sensations pulsed inside me, brand new ones. While she drove, I looked up my symptoms in the book, and we decided I must be experiencing false labor pains. But they wouldn't go away, and by the time of our first break at 11, I was feeling surpassing strange indeed. Are they contractions? the teacher asked me. How would I know? I'd never felt one before. As my due date was still three weeks away, I assumed they had to be something else. Then I discovered I was bleeding. The nurse-instructor insisted I go to the hospital immediately.

After we'd stopped at the house to pick up clothes and music and books ~ as I thought I still had another month, and first-time mothers were usually late, I'd not yet packed a bag ~ I was chagrinned to discover I would not be put under the care of a midwife, as planned, but under the M.D. on duty, due to the abrasion of my placenta, which was apparently causing the bleeding. Still fueled by caffeine and wired from lack of sleep and powered by whatever else was going on inside me, another kind of turning was upon me. The M.D. had the bedside manners of a nasty plumber, and I was damned if he would deliver my baby into this world. Our mutual antipathy gave me strength, and I determined to last out his 12-hour shift.

The bleeding stopped, I was given a room in the midwifery labor-and-delivery wing, and it appeared I was indeed going to drop this baby early. After eight months and one week, perhaps catalyzed by my double-espresso, Helen/Elijah was ready to leave confinement and join me on the outside. Or perhaps s/he had sensed my turning and knew I was ready to mother. All afternoon I listened to Richard Burton reciting John Donne, studied *Van Gogh in Arles* and took endless showers, waiting. My midwife was a man named Tom, the only male member of the team; he reminded me of a beloved former teacher who had died of AIDS, and I liked him at once. Brooke left to attend to details

~ no one except the baby was ready for today ~ and Kristi, who lived nearby, arrived to sit with me. We made lists of people to be called, and things that still needed doing. Somehow, I hadn't yet notified the adoption people, yet this omission did not occur to me.

Happy labor stories are all alike, but every labor is astonishing in its own way.

Approximately 24 hours after being admitted to the hospital, I gave birth to Elijah Max, 19 inches long, five and a half pounds, whose only apparent trouble was tachypnea, excessively rapid breathing sometimes present in early arrivals. Later I would learn this condition was not uncommon for babies born to antidepressant-popping mothers. As the hospital wanted to monitor him until he could breathe normally, he ended up in the nursery for five days until they let me bring him home, and I began my life as a mother.

Friends had cleaned the house and walked the dogs, making everything ready. The beautiful bassinette was parked in the living room beside my gliding rocking chair with its gliding ottoman, a group present from colleagues. Elijah had taken to my nipple with gusto, and the following days passed in an easy dreaminess. Baba stayed over and Steve brought us meals, my favorite Super-Dog Supreme Burritos from across town. Friends arrived to marvel. When I saw the red dog leash hanging on the ladderback chair, I didn't think of the big oak in the woods, waiting for me. Instead, I hooked it to Ralph's or Pete's collar, tucked Elijah in the Snuggly, and strolled the park with my baby and dogs, showing off to the dog-walking crowd I'd been studiously avoiding for so long. Some hadn't even known I was pregnant, but that didn't bother me. I walked in the meadows and avoided the trees. I put the psalms away.

The Week After Thanksgiving

In the psych ward, prisoners sported scrub outfits, while those of us who'd committed ourselves wore street clothes. The people in green had been ordered there by the courts; constantly they phoned their lawyers and probation officers, angrily waving paperwork and shouting long-distance. A strange division existed between those of us who'd chosen to be there, who believed that ward was our last hope, and those in green who resented every moment. They were not crazy, they screamed at their attorneys, demanding to be released at the soonest possible moment.

Once inside the locked doors, doors I had feared ever since my visit to another psych ward, at 12, to see my mother, instead of terrorized I felt calm. Peaceful. Here, I was safe ~ safe from my own despair and unable to harm my child, who was at home with our chosen-family grandparents. (My own parents did not know about my circumstances, nor would I ever enlighten them.) Every few hours, I went to the storage room to suction breast milk with an industrial-strength pump, delivered from the obstetrics floor for my use. Twice a day, Steve, the chosen-grandpa, came to the hospital to fetch my milk, bottled in sterile prescription drug containers, and I felt a bizarre satisfaction in the knowledge that while I was not safe to be around my son, at least I was providing him with healthy food from my body. (My friends called me The Dairy Queen, as I was so good at nursing. As in my lack of morning sickness, I took perverse pride in this biological happenstance; the same friend who had been ill much of her pregnancy now suffered from mastitis.)

Once inside the hospital, sure I could stay only one night, I immediately feared my looming departure. I couldn't imagine being away from Elijah for more than 24 hours even though it was my fear of hurting him that had pushed me to commit myself. I didn't want to ask my friends for too much kindness, unable to believe in their love for me and my child. But they prevailed, insisting I should spend at least a full day; my son would be fine, and so would they.

A week before, at my father's Manhattan apartment, I had stood on his twelfth floor balcony and contemplated throwing myself and my child over the railing. Six years later, to write these words still cuts me, but they are true. At that moment in my motherhood ~ nearly six months since I'd started a low dose of a new medication, exhausted in every possible way ~ I could imagine doing that deed: the child first, then me. Every night since his birth, my son needed his Dairy Queen at three-hour intervals. A good sleep was a memory I could no longer summon. With harsh objectivity, as if in a film I were directing, I envisioned the act clearly. Inside, my elderly father was reading *The New York Times* on his couch, the television blaring stock market news, which he would regard from time to time when he looked up from his paper. Depending on what the letters and figures scrolling across the screen revealed ~ I did not understand this language in any way ~ he would call up his broker and tell her to sell this or that, to buy this or that, in his businesslike, heavy German accent, extant despite fifty years in the United States.

As separate from him as I felt from myself, I wasn't conscious of what I knew to be depression, but I could replay the killing scene over and over as I gazed at the railing from my position frozen to the sliding glass doors. It was November's end, cold and sunny in New York, but the steam heat of his apartment made me sweat, so I'd stepped out to the balcony to get some air. A chaise lounge with white plastic cushions stretched beside me, a reminder that other seasons existed. Something wanted to pull me to the railing, so I didn't dare step one foot from the door. The balcony was small, perhaps 10 feet long and six feet wide. The view was nothing special: rooftops and a glimpse of Madison Avenue and 83rd Street. No one was visible, the huge metropolis apparently empty of humans from this elevation. No one would even see; my nearly deaf father wouldn't hear a thing.

In his late eighties, he was thrilled to be a grandparent again, as if my son somehow testified to his own virility. Now there was a new generation who would bear his name, as my sister took her husband's name, and my brother had not and would not reproduce. Elijah Max was named for my father's father as well as my maternal grandfather. Healthy and beautiful and alert, this grandbaby of his old age was his delight. My son's brown skin pleased my father: "He's a child of the twenty-first century," he said proudly, of which we were on the cusp in the penultimate month of 1999. He told me not to worry about money, about anything. He had great faith in me; already I had traveled to accept a prize for my writing, given a reading in the South, all as a high-powered single mother. And yet, there I was, stuck to the doors clutching my child, picturing the way my son and I would catapult over the edge into the void.

Upon my return to the West Coast, the world looked bleak. No one was in the next room to help, to reassure me not to worry about bills. My brightly painted kitchen failed to soothe. Each day seemed colder and damper than the one before. The dark rain of the Pacific Northwest fell without ceasing. Unlike the summer before, when I had craved the darkness, insulted by light, now I couldn't bear the unending gray skies that cover Oregon from October to March. Soon I would have to return to my job. How could I possibly function, stand in front of a group of students, and converse with colleagues when I could barely get through an hour without imagining the end of ends. Since summer, I had been seeing a therapist at Kaiser who was helpful, but not enough. Nothing was. On my mental movie screen, I kept replaying my baby and me flying off the edge of the balcony ~ again and again, like a rewound film one watches with sick humor as the fallen actors reel themselves up only to fall once more, and then repeat the action endlessly, like Sisyphus.

I called Steve and asked if he and Baba could come over right away. It seemed I was reaching a new low place, somehow even more deplorable than the pit of summer's darkness. This time, however, there was no impending date to relieve me ~ just unremitting horror. They came, and after pretending for a while that I was fine, I dared to tell them about the New York vision on my father's veranda. Perhaps the hospital was where I needed to be, they said, though I didn't want to go there. Steve and Baba accompanied my son and me to the therapist, where I had an appointment scheduled, and all of them together made the decision I was not safe at home. I resisted; I promised I would sign a contract not to hurt myself or my child, but please don't send me to the hospital. At the same time, a part of me wanted to go, to put behind me this horrible scene I was now directing ~ hysterical at Kaiser with my baby crying, dear friends pale and the therapist white with fear. She was in over her head, swimming in my deeps.

We drove home, got pajamas and a toothbrush while the therapist called admitting doctors and made possible my entry to the hospital. Back in my house, it was not unlike the flurry of three months before when I packed to give birth to Elijah ~ selecting music and books and whatever I thought I couldn't do without for a few days in the hospital. Only this time I'd be leaving Elijah behind. Baba and the baby stayed in the kitchen while Steve drove me across town. Did we talk? "You're doing the right thing," he told me.

Hospital lobbies look more like hotels than decades earlier, when I'd gone to see my mother in the psych ward, and then my brother in the same psych ward a few years later. This suburban hospital was fancier than Mt. Sinai in Manhattan, where I'd visited my brother in yet another psych ward. Paintings of sylvan Northwestern scenes adorned the walls. Big reading lamps abutted the couches. The bank of pay phones in mahogany reminded me of the Hilton downtown. People laughed and congregated on the comfortable sofas exchanging gossip, or reading newspapers, or chatting with patients in hospital gowns who looked surprisingly at ease.

After hugging Steve goodbye and thanking him over and over, I followed a nurse up to the 4th floor, where we had to be buzzed in, just like the floor to which my mother had been admitted. When I was 12, the idea of being a prisoner terrified me; I swore to myself I would never, ever be so weak and puny as to be incarcerated by psychiatrists. My brother's subsequent incarceration in more than one mental hospital only confirmed to me the necessity of my pledge. The glass through which the person behind the desk could check who wanted to enter was clear, while I remember the glass on the door of my mother's floor as having a wire grid – to prevent patients from breaking it, I suppose, to protect them from themselves.

This ward was painted in yellows, reds and blues; most of the patients wore civilian clothes. When the door locked into place behind us, and I was assigned a room with a thankfully empty second bed, I sat down and sighed with relief. It felt safe. I was not in charge here, not running the show of my life, and now the life of my child. I could sleep.

In the recreation room, a young girl the same age as my college freshmen and I began to speak. I felt strangely normal, wanting to help her, as if she were a student in my office. An older man who had also checked himself in, on the brink of becoming a minister, joined our conversation. Like me, he had disturbing ideas about the nature of existence, and didn't know if humans could be of any use on this planet. While reassuring the young girl of an important future before her, we shared her less articulate fears about the life ahead for all of us post-hospital.

18

In a room with a large table covered with paper and markers, I joined a group in which we were supposed to write affirmations. Although I despised this sort of activity, I forced myself to participate, if only to conceal my snobbery. In front of each person was an outline, coloring-book style, of a flower with long petals, on whose center we were to write our names and then pass to our right. Each petal would be filled in with a word or sentence that described one nice thing about the person the flower belonged to. As I didn't know anyone there, I felt phony and inadequate. People were writing sentences like "She has a sweet smile," or "he has nice eyes." It was a democratic group of patients ~ all races, ages, classes. Not everyone was depressed: some were manic, some angry. Some were catatonic. At the moment of feeling free of the burden of running my life, I was content just to be there, though I knew I needed some sort of pharmaceutical intervention to get me through the days to follow after I was buzzed out those doors.

My memory of speaking to the hospital psychiatrist in a tiny office comes to me as a flash of us sitting in a sort of confessional ~ though I've seen them only in films ~ with the shrink as priest and me as penitent. A redhead with thinning hair, he was puffy in middle age, pale and non-descript. To me, he seemed unhappy and disgruntled; surely being a psychiatrist in Kaiser's mammoth managed-care system was no one's first- choice post. Both of us remarked that the other looked familiar, and soon discovered we had both attended a Northwest Psychoanalytic Institute party some time back. In addition to upping and changing my meds, he told me it wasn't enough to live for my child.

This was a blow I hadn't foreseen. I had to live for myself, he insisted. Part of me thought his words simply a stupid male response; men didn't know how to love children. Men could create a child and not even know it, or walk away from a child they'd created, like the father of my son. Of course men couldn't know what children needed. (Neither do many women, it is true, but at that moment I wasn't thinking equitably.) He asked me if I thought my child was worthy of love. Yes of course, I said. He was worthy of all the good things in the world. And what of me? Was I? The question seemed absurd. Any infant was good; every infant deserved unconditional love. But what of me, he repeated.

What made me different from my child? Didn't I deserve love as well? The notion grated against an age-old understanding of my place in the universe. I was not an innocent infant; I was culpable in this fallen world. Despite my resistance to his idea, he insisted that I was in fact exactly like my child in worth and worthiness. My intellect could detect the logic in his statement, but everything in my 39 years of life rebelled against such heresy. Think about it, he insisted. You have a good mind. I want you to tell me in what way you are different from him in that regard. You were born exactly as he was born, "deserving unconditional love," he said, using my words. Whether you received it or not had to do with your parents, not you. In parting, he told me I would be a good candidate for psychoanalysis, and should think about calling the Institute when I was ready. Our thirty minutes had ended.

From down the corridor I heard a familiar voice and ducked into the kitchen area; I remembered then that Dr. M, who was married to a writer-friend of mine, worked at this hospital as a psychiatrist. Mortified, I hid behind the door, though he did not after all pass by. Cheeks red with embarrassment, I scolded myself for feeling ashamed. On the following weekend, mutual friends were having their annual Hanukkah celebration, and our families were invited. As I planned to go on living, I wanted to bring Elijah to that party, but there was something too bizarre about seeing him in here on Tuesday, in the psych ward as a patient, and then again on Saturday, lighting menorahs like normal people, eating latkes with friends. I remained in the kitchen until I heard him buzzed to the outside world.

Although I had briefly studied Kabala on my own and the summer before read the Psalms for solace, I did not have a sense of God. Daughter of an atheist Jew, I too became an atheist Jew, my life shadowed by the holocaust in which my father did not die, but which liberally cast survivor's guilt, even to the children of survivors, or at any rate, among my siblings, to me. After living through Scotland with the help of meds I had brought along for "just in case," I began to probe for something larger than nihilism. My father's creed of fact-based atheism could no longer sustain me. To base a life on history, to testify to what men do to other men and what they do to the earth, left me hopeless. My father seemed to live perfectly well with that knowledge; he traveled the world. He enjoyed art and a good laugh, word games and the crossword puzzle ~ in ink, of course. He liked to have dinner in the Trustees Dining Room at the Metropolitan across the street, where the waiters knew and liked him, welcoming him by name. The condition of the planet as it was had not and would not destroy him. "I'm not a pessimist," he insisted. "I'm a realist."

But for me, such realism led only to despair. From what I could tell, my mother and siblings had no particular belief systems. God was rarely, if ever, mentioned in my home. We were Jewish but not religious. At 9, I had proclaimed my atheism to myself and refused to say the word "God" in the pledge of allegiance, falling silent on that syllable. I stole a copy of Elie Wiesel's *Night* from my parents' bookshelves and read it secretly, knowing I was not supposed to possess such truths about humanity. I refused a religious education, fleeing on my bicycle the morning we were to register for Sunday School.

After Scotland, though, I knew I needed something bigger if I were to continue living, which I had once again decided to do, though not with any great intentionality. I found a kind of prayer in T.S. Eliot's *Four Quartets*, of which "Little Gidding" is the last. I read it every day, underlining and highlighting the parts I thought would help me stay alive. As I had Steve's old copy, given to me upon his retirement, I tried to puzzle out his marginalia, wondering what he had expected to find there. My guess was that he had not been looking for a poem to save him.

> The only hope, or else despair
> Lies in the choice of pyre or pyre~
> To be redeemed from fire by fire.
> "Little Gidding"

On its face, this stanza doesn't offer much by way of hope, yet somehow, I found it there, nestled in the lack of choice. To live in this world was to choose between pyres; it was good to know. "We only live, only suspire/Consumed by either fire or fire."

Upon my return from Scotland to Colorado, during my sabbatical year in a cabin high in the Sangres, the power went out in a windstorm my first night back. Around the cabin the trees soughed and scraped in the gusts racing across the meadow, making a terrible noise, the only noise. Huddled with my dog, the phones out as well, all I could do was ... pray. Pray to survive the night, pray that the windstorm would end without crashing the tall ponderosa onto the loft where I was sitting, where I felt safest despite being at the highest point in the cabin. The branches razored the windowsill, and I held my breath. I believed in Nature; I believed Nature was stronger than man and loved her for it. My father's worldview had no room for a power with more will than human beings, who were, to judge by most of history, largely monsters.

To believe in something in which there is no evidence for such belief – this is faith. Faith had never been part of my life. But from the night of the windstorm, in which hurricane-level gusts leveled houses and trees and telephone poles all over the valley, but left my rental intact, I began to allow myself to begin to entertain such belief. In something. Something bigger and stronger than humankind. I could not be an atheist any longer, though I had no new handy term to replace it. The wind testified to something. While men were killing Mother Nature with their strip mines and landfills, she could still strike back. And she would. When no one was looking or waiting. I found a strange joy in this new understanding, which persists today.

Back in the hospital, a place as unnatural as there could be, the doctor's insistence that I was as valuable a human being as my child seemed a theory beyond the realm of my understanding. I could not, in any empirical way, believe it. But I could pray to find faith in such a notion.

from "Little Gidding"
Not known, because not looked for
But heard, half-heard, in the stillness
Between two waves of the sea.
Quick now, here, now always –
A condition of complete simplicity
(Costing not less than everything)

Now

After my sojourn in the psych ward six years ago, I began to redefine myself. Previously, I perceived my life as that appropriate to a Depressed Person, and even if I wasn't depressed every minute of that life, my worldview was consistently dark. Like Woody Allen, I thought I couldn't be happy if anyone anywhere in the world was suffering. Or as my mother used to say, "only idiots are happy," and who wants to be an idiot? But since becoming a mother, and enjoying my stay on the fourth floor, and learning to pray, I have come to know joy. Not the manic pleasures I remembered from before, when it seemed as if any delight had to be swigged fast like a glass of ambrosia because its duration would surely be limited, like a two-day annual vacation in some exotic land. Rather, I have discovered joy in dailiness. I no longer see myself as that Depressed Person with a corresponding worldview. I have not returned to That Place, and don't plan to, though anything is possible. For the rest of my days, I will take my medication, which feels fine to declare, not the confession of a morally weak or ethically compromised soul.

Caring for another human being, loving my son, mothering him as best I can in the way I wish I had been mothered, has opened me up to the myriad delights of living. At the same time, I have not discarded my cynicism about the general nature of humanity, nor am I particularly hopeful about the planet's future. Many more Columbines have come to pass since 1999, including the three thousand dead on September 11th back home in New York, but despair has not returned to live with me. Recently, when a checkup revealed high cholesterol, I immediately changed my diet, discovering that my prodigious will could be channeled toward eliminating cheese, heavt a heretofore unimaginable feat. Because I wanted to live, to be around as long as possible to witness Elijah grow into the extraordinary human being he is becoming, I will do without havarti.

The world looks entirely different with my son in it. Always I had heard parents say things like, "you'll feel differently when you're a mother," but I never believed them. After all, plenty of parents commit suicide. Some harm their children, deliberately or otherwise. Some even kill them. But I don't want Elijah to live in the depressed shadow that was my home until so very recently. My father passed in 2000, and my mother is fading. Together, my siblings and I have found new cohesion in caring for our ever-difficult matriarch, communicating daily by email.

For the last two years, Elijah and I and our new dog, Rafe, have lived in the mountains in southern Colorado, in nearly perpetual sunlight ~ that is, when it isn't snowing or storming; I adore extremes of weather. My son learned to ride his bike on our dirt driveway far from any cars. Last summer, I was a backstage mother at a local performance of *Alice in Wonderland*, in which Elijah played Frog Footman. In Colorado, Columbine is the state flower; legions of it flank the creek nearby. I awaken before the sun and thrill to see a pair of coyotes fleeing daylight into the hills. Each morning in winter, I build a fire in the woodstove and start the coffee. I take my meds. After waking Elijah for school, our mutual routine begins: oatmeal, teeth brushing and lunch packing, the daily struggle over what jacket to wear, me always wanting the heaviest winter coat, he believing he can do with just a fleece. I thank God, Mother Nature and Father Sky as I drive down the hill to meet the schoolbus, the Sangres glowing pink in reflected sunrise.

Thou hast brought up my soul from the grave: thou hast kept me alive, that I
should not go into the pit.
Thou hast turned for me my mourning into dancing: thou hast put off my
sackcloth, and girded me with gladness.
from Psalm 30 (3) (11)

METAPHOR B. JONESTOWN 11/18/78
2005

"In order to talk ~ or even think ~ about almost anything, it is necessary to use metaphors," writes linguist George Lakoff and philosopher Mark Johnson in *Metaphors We Live By*. "Metaphor is not just a matter of words, but a major mode of thought."

When Americans and others talk about "drinking the Kool-Aid," they partake of metaphor often without acknowledgment. "Most of the time we are not even aware we are doing it, since most metaphorical thought is automatic and below the level of consciousness," says Lakoff.

Thirty-seven years after more than 900 human beings died at Jonestown after drinking poison mixed into a fruit drink concoction ~ mistakenly referred to as Kool-Aid, it was actually a cheaper powdered fruit concentrate called Flavor Aid ~ "drinking the Kool-Aid" has come to mean "swallowing the company line," in one definition, or "blindly going along with the majority without voicing one's opposition" in another.

For many Americans born after 1978, or those too young to have conscious memory of that time, "Jonestown" is a word without particular meaning, or perhaps it refers to towns in Pennsylvania and Texas. However, "drinking the Kool-Aid" is embedded in today's popular vocabulary. It is on its way to becoming what George Orwell, in his 1946 essay, "Politics and the English Language," called a "dead metaphor":

> A newly invented metaphor assists thought by evoking a visual
> image, while on the other hand a metaphor which is technically
> "dead" has in effect reverted to being an ordinary word and
> can generally be used without loss of vividness.

For readers of *The Jonestown Report*, I realize that the Kool-Aid metaphor is not dead at all, but a phrase that evokes with extreme vividness the fleshly children, elderly, families, and struggling individuals who participated in the final "White Night" ritual in Guyana. Some readers may visualize their family members and friends on the boardwalk near the vat, an oversized tin bucket in which death awaited those who had years before chosen to participate in a communal experience of living, a scene transforming before their horrified or numbed or depressed or resigned or resistant bodies into a communal experience of dying, on a humid afternoon in November 1978.

For today's Jonestown community ~ American and otherwise, scholars and artists and journalists in addition to Peoples Temple extended family and friends ~ drinking the Kool-Aid remains a literal and visceral description of an unfathomable moment in recent history.

Unfathomable, yet wholly and horribly real.

"Since our metaphors often hide important aspects of reality," writes Lakoff, "we need to know what they are."

What then does the Kool-Aid metaphor eclipse?

It disappears 909 lives of accumulated experience and wisdom. It conceals yet another example in a long line of America's utopian experiments-turned-dystopia, in which ends cannot justify means. It hides what we, collectively, as a culture of diverse peoples of the 21st century, wish to forget.

In the pavilion at Jonestown, above the bodies of the dead and Jim Jones's empty throne, photographers captured the sign reading "Those who forget the past are condemned to repeat it," philosopher George Santayana's celebrated dictum regarding our duty to study history. The irony of this statement crowning the hundreds of corpses is not lost on any viewer of these images.

And yet, endlessly, we forget the past, and repeat it.

"SCATOLOGY OR ESCHATOLOGY?"
1995

As I bent over the toilet in a highway rest stop, in a dream exactly resembling reality, Debbie from grade school asked me this intense, theological wordplay question while I examined my feces as if they were tea leaves. Why a highway restroom? Why Debbie, a girl from elementary school decades and decades earlier, whose chief role in my memory up until now was her making fun of my best friend, who had a prominent pimple in the center of her face. "What's that balloon on your nose?" asked Debbie in real life, my friend turning red as a Central Park helium inflatable.

Debbie is black; I am white. Debbie was an amazing athlete, funny and charismatic. I was chubby, one of the worst athletes in school, proverbially last to be picked for teams, and more than a little in awe of her. Her boldness frightened me, as she seemed to fear nothing and no one, and evidently felt free to voice her opinion anytime, anywhere.

Scatology I knew, from studying 18th century literature in graduate school: the study of shit. Eschatology, which is pronounced just the same as the other - ology after the extra first syllable, I had to look up. I knew it had something to do with "last things." The official definition was "the part of theology concerned with death, judgment, and the final destiny of the soul and of humankind."

"Wow, what a great dream!" said my therapist. "Let's get started."

In my thirties, then, I was creating a new life as a non-depressed person, complete with anti-depressants and twice-weekly therapy with an excellent psychiatrist, with whom, of course, I had fallen wholeheartedly in love. Now the dream is twenty years old, yet I still remember how much he loved a juicy nighttime reverie, replete with literary wordplay.

In certain ways, Debbie's question ~ she must have been standing on the toilet seat in the next stall, for her head suddenly appeared above me ~ seems to me the basic question of life. Is it just shit? Or is there a deeper meaning, that, if excavated, will take us past excrement into theology?

My dream's pairing of the two ideas was not original; I was already familiar with the "Shit Happens" list of religious explanations of why it happens, and to whom. I had a few favorites, of course: my own tradition of Judaism's "Why does this shit always happen to us?" as well as Hinduism's "This shit has happened before," and the Stoic's "This shit is good for me."

The dream has stayed with me because of its humor, its wordy wit, and something fundamentally profound about my childhood schoolmate's question. In this fifty-plus stage of life, I keep encountering shit in its literal form: the expected diapering of my infant born late in my life – that was ordinary. But later, while my mother was dying, suffering from ulcerative colitis or what she liked to call "My Crohn's" [Disease], I spent hours cleaning up after her: in toilets, around toilets, behind toilets, in carpet, on nightgowns, Depends, commodes, everywhere.

In my cabin in the Colorado mountains, off the grid where we moved eight years ago, I inherited a dysfunctional compost toilet which necessitates several hours each month with rubber gloves, the transport of human scat amidst scads of cow manure, as my acreage is not fenced and the neighbors' herds roam freely, especially attracted, for no reason I can pinpoint, to my little cabin out in the hills.

After my mother died, we moved into a house with real plumbing. I assumed my preoccupation with shit ~ if it was indeed neurosis or obsession ~ was, so to speak, at its natural end.

But now, my son, entering adolescence, is constantly stopping up our water-saving toilet because his shit is too big! He won't eat vegetables or whole grains either. At last, back on the grid of sewers and endless running water spouting from taps, I seem to spend way too much time plunging the toilet. Yes, he plunges too, but I'm better at it. He will give up, and me, I know I have to keep at it or we cannot get on with our lives.

Scatology or eschatology?

I tell myself it's good for my soul to deal with excrement on a nearly daily basis, as it keeps me humble, reminds me of the commonality between us and animals, my son and me, the dogs and the cows, etc. Yet others manage to live their lives without these constant reminders of last things. For Catholics, "If shit happens, you deserve it." Maybe in another life I was a Papist? For the Calvinist: "Shit happens because you don't work." Perhaps all this shit is punishment for taking early retirement?

Freud said the infant produced feces for the parents as a gift; for the child, it has to be perceived as a present since the mother oohs and aahs over the final product, proof of health and wealth ~ a highly valued offering.

Hercules had to clean the Augean Stables of centuries of offal. With the help of the gods, he accomplished this unimaginable feat. Then there is the apocryphal story of the young cowboy using his pitchfork, searching and searching through enormous piles of horse dung. "I know there's a pony in here somewhere," he says earnestly to his interlocutor's question of what is he doing and why.

What was my response to Debbie, the athletic interrogator of third grade fame? In the dream, I didn't say anything, too awed by her question. Perhaps it would be something about destiny embodied inside the porcelain throne: scatology and eschatology, both eternally present.

FATHOM THESE EVENTS:
JONESTOWN, A NOVEL
2004

"It will take more than small minds, reporters' minds, to fathom these events. Something must come of this. Beyond all the circumstances surrounding the immediate event, someone can perhaps find the symbolic, the eternal in this moment ~ the meaning of a people, a struggle ~ I wish I had time to put it all together, that I had done it. I did not do it. I failed to write the book. Someone else, others, will have to do this."

~ attributed to Richard Tropp, Jonestown anonymous document

Sangre de Cristo range, southern Colorado, Wet Mountain Valley, 9,100 feet, 35 acres, half a mile from neighbors, 5 1/2 miles of dirt and 11 miles of pavement to town, two hours to nearest airport, four hours to major airport and metropolis, myself and my son and my dog, and antelope, coyote, hummingbirds, red-tail hawks, mule deer, Rocky Mountain bluebird, plagues of mice and biting red ants. No land line (sometimes the cell-phone works); solar; propane; candles; kerosene. Completely off the grid, as they say. Here, I have chosen to spend the last year reading everything about Jonestown I am able to find, listening to Jim Jones' voice on dozens of tapes, seeking solace in the land and sky.

Spring 2004. University of North Dakota Annual Writers' Conference, where I am writer-in-residence for a week, giving a reading of my new novella, "The Closer You Were, the Less You Knew," about a New York family (not my own) and its history, which happens to collide with the events of September 11th, 2001. During the 1980s, two daughters out of three join a cult in the Southwest, and the parents find a deprogrammer to "rescue" them. The hired man discloses that he has lost his own daughter in Jonestown. Otherwise, Peoples Temple is tangential to the story. After the reading, a friend comes up to me in tears, confiding he has a colleague whose two sisters and nephew died in Jonestown.

November 18, 1978: 918 dead; five murdered for sure; an hour on dirt from

Port Kaituma; 26 hours by boat from Georgetown; an hour by plane from Georgetown; no phone at all; limited radio ~ as far as you can get from the grid.

Summer 2004. Portland, Oregon. Getting ready for my sabbatical in Colorado, where I plan, after five years of preparation, to begin my new novel, *Hippie Ruins*, about a commune in Huérfano County which began in the 1960s and whose residents, though dwindling, persist, surviving the pressures of poverty, bad health, growing old without health insurance. At Powell's Books, where I am shopping for research material, I find myself drifting from "Communes" to "Cults," its neighbor category down the aisle. I find several books on Jonestown and decide, amid the sensationalist titles and grainy photos from Guyana, to postpone *Hippie Ruins* for another time, and write my novel about Jonestown instead.

Cult Controversies; Strange Gods: The Great American Cult Scare; Cults: Faith, Healing and Coercion; Communes and Cults; Death of a Cult Family; The Suicide Cult; The Cult That Died; The Cult Experience; Cults in America; Cults and New Religious Movements; Tragic End of a Cult; The New Religious Cults; The Cult Experience: Salvation or Slavery.

Spring 2005. I'm hiking with the dog on the bald hills of the Wet Mountain range, a French actor reading Camus's *Le Myth de Sisyphe* in my ears, sometimes carrying the book in French, sometimes in English, sometimes both, sometimes completely textless, as I try to absorb the words. I feel sure that if I read/hear this essay enough times, enlightenment will follow. *Il n'y a qu'un problème vraiment sérieux; c'est le suicide.* ("There is but one truly serious philosophical problem, and that is suicide," trans. Justin O'Brien.) This opening line of the essay was written in 1942, when the writer was a Resistance fighter against fascism, not only that of the Nazis but of his own government, the Vichy collaborationists. A mile from the cabin, I find two old troughs, constructed of heavy wooden slabs, perfect for the flowerboxes I plan for summer blooms. How to get them home? There is no road, so I find a rope and drag them, one at a time, up and down the cactus-speckled slopes, without benefit of wheels or pulleys; they are too heavy for me to lift. I have to laugh at myself, enacting Sisyphus in the flesh. Is this the task of the Jonestown novelist?

More Camus. Machiavelli's *Prince*. Orwell. Campbell's *The Hero With A Thousand Faces*. James's *Varieties of Religious Experience*. *Moby Dick*. Dostoyevsky. More and more Dostoyevsky.

Spring 2005. An email arrives with the name of a major Jonestown writer as the sender, and the message line is: Jonestown Novel. "Dear Dr. Dawid," it reads. "We have heard through the grapevine that you are writing a novel related to Jonestown" and goes on to offer me archival assistance. And access to recordings of Jim Jones and the people of Peoples Temple. I need to hear their voices so that I may be a proper conduit. Eagerly, like a child sending away for a prize, I mail a check for 20 cassettes, for starters.

Primo Levi's *Survival in Auschwitz*. Terrence des Pres's *The Survivor*. Jean Amery's *At the Mind's Limits: Contemplations by a Survivor on Auschwitz and Its Realities*; Steiner's *Treblinka* and Wiesel's *La Nuit*. Nine hours of *Shoah*.

Planting or painting while Jim Jones speaks into my ear of Socialism and sky gods. To counter the voice, the deadly inevitable end, I must create, must grow. A few packets of seeds turn into a dozen, then two dozen. Jones berates Stanley and some anonymous "intellectual" says the fascists are coming, and now they won't let Black people into Canada. I paint flowerpots I've recycled from the detritus of my small town's café. Cerulean blue, electric lime, stopsign red. Sometimes I agree with Jones's words: yes, racism remains the scourge of our nation, thirty years later; yes, the poor are overlooked and uncared for, the elderly forgotten or ripped off, the children ignored while Capitalism waltzes on, the ship of state capsizing every day. John Deere green, woodstove black, lemon yellow. "Dad teaches us daily to think for ourselves," insists one of the Jonestown residents. Furiously, I plant nasturtium, bachelor buttons, lupine, hollyhock, California poppies, foxglove, lavender, dill, basil, tomatoes and more tomatoes.

Beyond Jonestown; *The Secret of Jonestown*; *Jonestown Massacre*; *Jonestown and the Manson Family*; *Jonestown in American Cultural History*; *Unraveling the Mysteries of Jonestown*; *Hearing the Voices of Jonestown*; *The Untold Story of Jonestown*; *The Jonestown Letters*; *The Need for a Second Look at Jonestown*; *A Sympathetic History of Jonestown*; *The Untold Story of What Happened Before – and Beyond – Jonestown*; *Jonestown & Other Madness*; *Remembering Jonestown*; *Surviving Jonestown*; *Behind*

Jonestown; From Babylon to Jonestown; The Assassination of Representative Leo J. Ryan and the Jonestown, Guyana Tragedy; Making Sense of the Jonestown Suicides; From Jonestown to Heaven's Gate; The Jonestown Tragedy, What Every Christian Should Know; The Children of Jonestown; The True Story Behind the Jonestown Massacre, including connections to the Kennedy and King assassinations; A Jonestown Survivor's Story; The Jonestown Guyana Holocaust of 1978; Was Jonestown a CIA Medical Experiment?

Hiking down the arroyo to the creek, Walkman in my ears, I listen as Joseph Campbell lectures on the facets of the hero. Is Jim Jones a hero? Are his followers heroic? What of the quest for self-knowledge? Did he or they achieve it? Meanwhile, monsters and tyrants figure in every myth. Like the Minotaur, Jim Jones hails from Crete (Indiana). His mother nurtures visions of grandeur for her offspring ~ heroic, outsized fantasies.

Hold Hands and Die!; Deceived; Our Father, Who Art in Hell; Let Our Children Go!; Six Years With God; A New World Tragedy; The Broken God.

Who will populate my novel? So many possibilities: Hyacinth, Odell, Marceline, Lew, "Bonny," Eugene, Harriet and Dick (Richard), Rose, the Doctor, the Nurses. The dog and I travel the cow path, finding ragged cooking pots ravaged by wind and age, a pioneer washtub, cowboy coffee tins; all this flotsam of dead homesteaders will float back into use as containers for vegetables and fragrant floral mixes to attract butterflies and hummers.

People's Temple, People's Tomb; Peoples Temple and Black Religion; The Inside Story of the Peoples Temple Sect and the Massacre in Guyana; Life and Death in the People's Temple; A Sociological History of Peoples Temple.

At night, my five-year-old son and I watch movies while I hook rugs of hot pink, burnt orange, mustard yellow and a panoply of greens. I must have color to offset the horror, the recycled photos of bodies rotting in the jungle, corpses in metal boxes sitting on the runway, awaiting a flight home, awaiting identification. Will my book identify them? Can I?

The Strongest Poison; Seductive Poison.

Everything in the world represents some aspect of Jonestown, or so it eems to me. George W. Bush and his fear-mongering; the bombers in Iraq and the

London Tube; all the animals in *Animal Farm*; the population of Narnia and nearly every children's movie and book which grapple with the meaning of good, the menace of evil. Ahab leads his crew to certain death in his quest for vengeance against the Leviathan, a monster embodying all his demons. The sailors go along because they have to; out on the Pequod, far from the world, they follow. Only Ishmael survives to testify.

The Tragedy of Jim Jones; Jim Jones: Christian or Antichrist? Charlatan or Communist?; The Untold Story of the Rev. Jim Jones; The Life and Death of Jim Jones; Jesus & Jim Jones; The Story of the Layton Family and the Reverend Jim Jones.

Months pass, and the novel evolves in my head, chronicled in my process notes. The books and tapes keep arriving to my post office box. While listening to Jim harangue Marceline, I grit my teeth. Suddenly I hear myself cry out, "I hate you!" to this man who calls himself "Dad," who seems a copycat Father Divine after I finish reading the same biography Jones had on his shelf, the 1953 edition of Sara Harris's book. I cry when Sharon Amos's children talk about why they should die for socialism.

Salvation and Suicide; On Suicide: A Discourse on Voluntary Death; Le Suicide; Suicide in Guyana; The Suicide Cult; Making Sense of the Jonestown Suicides.

My son has brown skin. I am a Jew, a third of my European family killed in the camps. Jim Jones is right to distrust the government ~ then and now. The so-called Patriot Act makes my library record suspect: amazingly, I can get Huey P. Newton's "Revolutionary Suicide" on interlibrary loan here at this tiny county branch. A news junkie, I find each day's headlines overwhelmingly dire.

The Nation; The New Yorker; The Atlantic Monthly; Harper's; Times Literary Supplement; Mother Jones; Speakeasy; The New York Times; Ode; Truthout.

And yet. As the monsoon season fills the huge skies with cumulonimbus, and the thunder crackles across the range, my flower troughs burst in voluminous blossom. Electrifying colors glisten in the rain. While the dog and I hike, voices whisper in my ear.

THE FOX BREAKS THE CODE

2000

In his will, my 87-year-old lawyer father included the proviso that the definition of grandchildren who would benefit from his estate included, in addition to any extant grandchildren, "any child born to any of my three children up to and including nine months from the date of my death." What was he thinking? That one of us would go out and impregnate or get pregnant within 24 hours of his passing?

Probably, he was thinking of me.

Unlike my siblings, I actually would do something like that. (Though I didn't, too busy with my one-year-old son, whom I'm raising alone.) The mystery behind such a clause leads me to the box of condoms I found in the medicine cabinet when I cleaned out his apartment a few months after the memorial service, over which I presided, my milk leaking as I spoke from the podium. My siblings weren't interested in the contents of my father's Fifth Avenue co-op; me, I knew there'd be juicy information, perhaps in code. The ripped open Trojan box, designed to hold 12 prophylactics, contained only 11.

In a drawerful of correspondence, I found a slew of cards addressed to my dour, sour father dated a few years previous, from one Gloria Greenberg on East 88th Street. Each message contained some sort of thank you ~ for flowers, a night at the theater, the card he'd sent her, and for being such a wonderfully kind and generous man on her birthday. What were his gifts, I wondered. Dinner out? Jewels? Art? From the handwriting, I deduced that Mrs. Greenberg ~ she used the title on her return address ~ was close to his age; each letter was carefully formed, slanting just so, her numerals curvaceous. Clearly, she'd studied *penmanship*, a skill dropped from the latter twentieth century curriculum. Naturally, I was glad to discover that this romance ~ how many were there? ~ had not been with some young gold-digger, though she might have been an old one.

But could elderly Mrs. Greenberg be responsible for the missing condom?

The potency date on the box had long since expired. Surely, she would not be risking pregnancy. Would my father have worried about AIDS? I could picture him reminding himself, in his no-nonsense way, "no point in risking a sexually transmitted disease," even in his 80s. But Mrs. Greenberg's refined cursive led me to believe their tryst was chaste.

If not Gloria, then who? I considered the possibility of a prostitute but was unable to imagine their point of contact. Times Square? A call girl? Some indigenous woman on his many travels?

Gloria's letters spanned six months. What had become of Mrs. Greenberg's and my father's affair? And did she need to know her former beau was deceased?

Later, I wrote, but my card returned to me: "No Such Occupant."

In another family, siblings might consult. Collectively, they might decide to shield their widowed mother from information she need not have. Over a drink and after a bawdy laugh or two, they might decide to burn the letters, cremating the tale of Gloria and their randy old dad, her words in ashes like the deceased patriarch himself. In some families, the death of a father might precipitate change, perhaps engender new channels of communication, but these did not open in mine.

I did not disclose the mystery of the twelfth condom, nor the existence of Gloria's cards, which now burrow in my study, hidden among innocuous correspondence for my child to unearth one day. Honoring his tradition, I hoard my father's secrets, disclosing only to the page, not to flesh, telling strangers, never my own.

Other imbrications: my mother had an abortion in those illegal days after my brother's birth, which came right after my sister's birth, both unplanned. The existence of the abortion was related to my married sister upon the joyous disclosure of her first pregnancy, by way of some obscene warning from my mother about the perils of bearing children before one was ready. Not knowing what to do with such information, my sister unburdened my mother's secret to me, though not to my brother. Did he know he was a "mistake"? Did my father know of the abortion? My grandmother? Or had my mother nursed this tale in private for 25 years, the words leaking out when she could contain them no longer? Was the abortion confession an oblique directive? It haunted, because the child first born to my sister was to die before his second birthday of an incurable, undetectable genetic disease. Did my mother know my sister told me? My sister forgot she did.

A few years before his death by heart attack ~ his fifth ~ my father nearly died of diabetes. A West Coaster, I'd been in Kentucky for a conference and had just returned home Sunday night to a bevy of messages on my answering machine regarding my father's dire condition in a New York hospital. The friend who'd picked me up from the airport, Steve, graciously returned the dog to the dog sitter and me to the airport, where, a few hours later, I caught a red-eye. In the morning, my recovering father, still woozy in post-op (after surgery for a superficial wound whose complications nearly killed him) looked at me, the first to arrive ~ though the East Coast family lived only a few hours away ~ and said, "You look like a fox." Had the anesthesia skewed his vocabulary? Or did I, in the dawning light, resemble the actual animal? Or was he using the vernacular, the term for a sexy woman? Did he think I was my mother? To whom could I confide this word?

Later that visit, with my father out of intensive care and clearly on the mend, I suddenly managed the arithmetic regarding the number of months between my parents' marriage ~ about whose actual date they had always been fuzzy ~ and my sister's birth. "Dad, was Mom pregnant when you got married?" In his hospital pallor, my father laughed loud and hard. "My god!" (Which, in his accent, sounded like "gott!") "Did it take you all these years to figure that out?"

How many other secrets, like that one, shimmer openly? And why hadn't my siblings, over the decades, ever questioned a three-month courtship and an anniversary never celebrated? Me, it took 37 years, but my elder sister and brother never asked. Years later, at my mother's deathbed, when I revealed this fact to my sister, she was flummoxed.

Why did I tell her?

To blame her, indirectly, for our parents' miserable marriage that, despite an unofficial separation, went on and on until they died, each alone? In 1953, my mother would not have thought to raise a child by herself. Did she then contemplate an abortion instead of marriage? Did my father forbid it? In his refugee's haste to start an American family, could the pregnancy have been the result of rape?

From his apartment, I took boxes and boxes of papers ~ letters, finances, notes scrawled in German shorthand. Inscrutable, he was, like the sprawling, handwritten notebook from Berlin in the 1930s, a palimpsest I imagine I might puzzle out one day if I could find a translator for his nearly illegible sentences.

A lover once complained I left every container open ~ not only the toothpaste but the milk carton, back door and front gate. Why is it I can't bear locks, and rooms without windows? My sister and brother close themselves up, impervious. Aren't they curious about our father's secret life? About mine?

Unlike them, I believe the unspoken and unwritten can be deciphered, each according to her need. In the language of his will, my father was telegraphing me:

"Beloved: you are still young. Make another life."

QUEEN OF THE DOGS
1998

That year, I summered in Martin Canyon, Huérfano County. There I read and wrote in a tiny one-room house not far from Martin Creek, to which I repaired every day to read, my feet dangling in the cool waters while the sun burned. I arrived with Ralph, my beloved Aussie/Border Collie/Bernese (not Burmese, as I had initially heard the breed named) Mountain Dog mix. For two weeks of that summer, I dog sat two canine friends, the pets of grad school classmates, one living in Alamosa, the other in Denver.

Leia (as in Princess), was small and scrappy, with a ferocious bark. Rosie, the runt of her Rhodesian Ridgeback litter, was an oversized galumphing girl, cinnamon-colored and silly. Now I had a train of three on my walks to the creek, past the beaver pond, where we watched on full moons the master engineers at work. I marveled at their enormous dams, the way they did their work with purpose and without waste.

That summer of 1998 was my last as a freewheeling, childless writer. Planning to become pregnant that fall, I wanted to take advantage of my ultimate solo vacation, soon to recede into memory along with childhood and other eras. Yet, I became a maternal shepherdess to my flock of canines, Ralph, Leia and Rosie accompanying me everywhere, even within the confines of my one-room adobe, from toilet to fridge to bed. Then another dog showed up, arriving unannounced one day with a sweet smile and beguiling eyes: I felt all the symptoms of being in love.

After local inquiries, I discovered the still-nameless dog "belonged" to a couple who lived nearby but unseen, in a trailer beneath a multitude of cottonwoods, upstream. They did nothing for "their" dog except take nominal ownership; when I brought him over the following day to say he had been hanging around my house, they looked irritated. "Oh, there's Pete," they said, unhappily. I saw no dog bowl, no water vessel. The woman threw a pizza crust at him out the window. As I left, heavy-hearted, Pete followed me. "He's following me," I called back, and the man begrudgingly found a chain with which to tie Pete to a tree.

He was some kind of Australian cattle dog, part Kelpie, who had never lived inside a dwelling or been in a car. Clearly, he had never been loved. I told myself sternly that I already had a dog, would soon have a child, and absolutely could not take Pete into my home. But he was already inside.

The couple didn't keep barking Pete on the chain for long. Immediately, he returned, and I started feeding him, knowing what I was doing without admitting it. I couldn't let him starve, after all. Upon entering the house for the first time, he peed on the wall but quickly learned the difference between outside and inside.

Now my retinue contained four dogs, happily tripping behind me to my mornings at Martin Creek. When a friend saw us walking down the road, he named me "Queen of the Dogs." I liked them all, but was ready when Rosie and Leia went home to their families, leaving me with beloved Ralph and the adoring Pete.

Summer's end approached. If I asked the couple to allow me to take Pete home to Oregon, they might say sure, go ahead. But some people who abuse their dogs ~ as with their children ~ maintain an "ownership" of that damaged or neglected creature that precludes other adults' involvement. It would be as if I were implying with such a request: "You obviously don't know how to take care of Pete."

This was manifestly true.

"And I do." Also true.

Instead, I kidnapped Pete, and drove my two boy dogs back to Oregon, Pete insistently trying to grab the windshield wipers from inside his perch on the passenger seat.

I wish I had a happy ending to supply.

The following January, when I was 3 months' pregnant, Pete bit me across the face one night because I picked him up, a gesture he never trusted, sending me to the emergency room for 15 stitches on both cheeks. It was my fault, I told myself: he warned me by growling, yet I continued to carry him in my arms, as if he were the baby-to-be.

Others thought I should get rid of Pete then. I couldn't.

But soon after my son was born, Pete decided, while Elijah and I had left the house, to tear his infant-smelling quilt into a hundred pieces.

That warning I listened to.

It was one thing for me to have a few scars, another for a jealous dog to rip into my helpless child. "He's wild," my vet told me. "He'll never be civilized."

No shelter would take him when I told the truth about my 15 stitches, not even the no-kill ones. Inevitably, I held him in my arms while the very kind technician at the county shelter injected him with death.

Sobbing, I listened to her insist I was doing the right thing as she recounted too many stories of dogs abandoned and tortured. In contrast, Pete had experienced more than a year of love in his life, she said, a gift I had offered and fulfilled for as long as I possibly could.

ARRIVAL
2004

Despite having traveled abroad and lived in diverse places ~ London, Australia, and a 1951 yellow GMC schoolbus in Northern California ~ these days I don't want to travel farther than I can see. From my tiny cabin, set in a bowl of the Wet Mountains with a head-on view of the Sangre de Cristos, I see far.

On a crystalline day like today, when the temperature's zero and the light so bright on the snow I wear sunglasses inside, I glimpse the Huajatollas, (named "Breasts of the World" by the Utes, "Spanish Peaks" by the conquistadors), 60 miles to the south, and the Collegiates far to the north. No trees obscure my sightline. Mountains and me, my dogs, my son, the sun, and wind. Sky and clouds and nobody else. Here, we live at what feels like the top of the world. When I drive home, up the steep rocky incline called "Little Bad Hill" ~ not to be confused with "Big Bad Hill" further south ~ I leave mundane troubles behind for the heights, where ideas emerge sharper, like the spires of the Crestone Needle due west, and emotions richer, like the plumed cumulonimbus roiling up and anvilling out in summer thunderstorms. Here, I can think, feel, and breathe, unencumbered.

Twenty years ago, on a weekend winter escape from graduate school at the University of Denver, a friend and I drove three hours south, then west up 96, climbing the soaring Hardscrabble Canyon, and, not long afterward, setting eyes for the first time on the Wet Mountain Valley, its great expanse extraordinarily unscathed by human intent. The small towns of Silver Cliff and Westcliffe claim the valley floor at 7,888 feet, and abandoned mines speckle the hills east of town, but then, as now, one can see far and wide, as the aboriginal peoples did, without feeling fettered by what Huck Finn sardonically called "sivilization." One feels small here, like the miniscule figures in Asian landscape paintings the viewer has to hunt to find. Appropriately, one feels one's humility in the natural world.

We spent a weekend with our typewriters (the manual kind) and our dictionaries (French, Swedish) translating poetry and breathing the clear cold air of a place without traffic or traffic lights, watching through our binoculars red-tailed hawks and kestrels riding thermals. For the first time, I'd encountered a land in which I felt free. Free of constraints on my thinking as well as liberated from ordinariness.

One week before, my friend and I huddled in the night at her Washington Park apartment, terrorized, as a helicopter circled over, buzzing the usually quiet corner again and again, a policeman's amplified voice demanding the person being chased come out in the street and give himself up. Running footfalls echoed on the spotlit sidewalks. Silent with fear, we trembled in darkness, dreading that whoever was fleeing the law might break into this ground floor flat to hide from his pursuers. Thankfully, he did not.

Although I was born on the East Coast, spent most of my adulthood on the West Coast, and always thought of myself as an "ocean person," in my thirties and now forties, I find my solace landlocked, here in the Sangres. For two summers, I sojourned on the Oregon Coast after moving to Portland in 1990; then Colorado summoned me back. In the Huérfano and Wet Mountain Valleys, I soon found myself renting cabins and adobes, my Honda packed tight with books and typewriter ~ not to be replaced by a computer until the twenty-first century. After spring finals, I couldn't wait to drive the 1,500 miles, to arrive where I could read and write: no longer commentary on student papers, but my own prose.

I do not miss the ocean. I find the Northwest's forests claustrophobic, the endless moisture heavy on my lungs. Moss grows on the roof of Portland bungalows as if to seal their inhabitants hermetically from light, and it never, ever thunders. Here, now, the sun rises in the East-facing window over my bed, waking me, and sets out the dining table window. The coyotes serenade us to sleep. Finally, I am where I want to be.

WHAT THEY CHOSE

2007

"If God does not exist, Kirilov is god.
If God does not exist, Kirilov must kill himself.
Kirilov must therefore kill himself to become god.
The logic is absurd, but it is what is needed."

Albert Camus, *The Myth of Sisyphus* (italics mine)

Like the Guyanese intellectual, Virgil, one of the four protagonists in my novel, currently titled *Resurrection City*, I seek understanding in literature, philosophy, and art. Unlike him, I have not given up, nor shall I. What I pursue is clarity. Not logic or order. Certainly not beauty.

In his endlessly fascinating essay, "The Myth of Sisyphus" ~ which Virgil reads and re-reads ~ Albert Camus, philosopher and novelist, Resistance warrior and ethical soul, analyzes Dostoyevsky's existential hero of *The Possessed*, the engineer Kirilov. Though I confess I have yet to finish *The Possessed*, I see in Camus' description of Kirilov an approximation of the Jonestown suicides of November 18, 1978.

In my reading, Kirilov does not stand for Jim Jones alone, but rather all the adults who chose to die and to kill others who could not or would not kill themselves. This approach diverges from the psychological explanation of paranoid delusions and/or deep depression. It removes international politics from the equation as well as the criminal repercussions of that afternoon's murders of the U.S. Congressman and others on the runway at Port Kaituma.

Much has been made of Jones' claims over the years to be god, or to have replaced what he called the "sky god" with Socialism as an alternative deity. The stories that he supposedly stomped on the Bible ~ telling his followers to stop paying attention to it and to focus on him instead ~ may be apocryphal. What seems most relevant is Jones' embrace of that "sky god" in the last hours of Jonestown.

"For months I've tried to keep this thing from happening," he says on the final tape, "but now I see that it's the will of the Sovereign Being that this happened to us."

Suddenly, god or God ~ the "Sovereign Being" ~ is no longer inside him or inside Peoples Temple, but rather an outside entity over which he and the others have no agency. It is as if, in those last minutes, the Jones and Jonestown that determined their own world had evaporated, and, at this moment in his speech, Jones surrenders to the omnipotent God of his youth, the same God he had pointedly disavowed during the intervening decades.

* * * * *

"If God exists," writes Camus, "all depends on him and we can do nothing against his will. If he does not exist, everything depends on us."

The roughly one-third of Jonestown's population consisting of adults of sound mind and body who took their lives willingly ~ as opposed to those who were forcibly injected ~ are responsible for their acts. They cannot evade their terrible responsibility, nor should they. Neither Jones nor Dr. Schacht nor the nurses or guards forced their hands to self-annihilation.

In the anthology, *In A Dark Time*, Drs. Robert Jay Lifton and Nicholas Humphrey write, "For it is the privilege, and the burden, of human beings to have knowledge of good and evil, and free will: when we come to judgment we come to it *on our own account*, according to how we have lived our earthly lives." So for those who chose to die, whether imagining they might become god or rather to escape the horrors of November 18, 1978, they did so on their own account, with all the burden and privilege that choice confers. They chose death, and in their aftermath, we who remain have no choice but to live in the terrible wake of that decision.

BABYSITTER GOES TO WAR
2007

Back in the liberal land of Portland, I wheeled my son in his stroller to anti-war protests before the invasion of Baghdad, our placard reading "Education not War," beneath a Picasso-like dove. Surrounded by like-minded citizens, we paraded through the green streets of the city, many of us as distant from the military as to the moon.

In our new home of Westcliffe, Colorado, the military permeates everyday life. Memorial Day is the year's most important holiday; the veterans occupy a respected role in the community, with major floats in all parades, which rumble down Main Street to protracted applause. Do I clap? Sometimes. Mostly, I try to avoid attending, not to demonstrate for my son such unquestioned reverence for war.

Volunteering at the public school, I hear a first-grader proudly declare, "When I grow up, I want to be a soldier in Iraq like my uncle." I cringe but say nothing in the middle of "World Explorer" class, reading from a children's biography of Toussaint L'Ouverture, hero of Haiti's revolutionary war. I celebrate the insurgents' 1804 overthrow of the French government ~ ridding the island of slavery over sixty years before the Civil War ended the practice here ~ but simultaneously acknowledge the bloody effort required to achieve that freedom. This boy sees all wars as the same: a test of male valor and patriotism. The bell rings, and I have no time to explain the difference between the modern era's sole overthrow of slavery and the United States' military invasion of Iraq.

My son's last male babysitter is now in Afghanistan. With his earrings, soft voice and long hair, he seemed an unlikely candidate to volunteer. An 18-year-old boy, humiliated by the breakup of his first romance, he decided to enlist for lack of a suitably dramatic alternative. The former girlfriend, a scholarship student at university, would be sorry, wouldn't she, if he got injured or killed! Unfortunately, he is like many non-academic boys with few options after high school in a community where "service" is always defined militarily.

Now Elijah's current babysitter, a high school senior, contemplates signing up after graduation. One Sunday, after building Legos all afternoon with my seven-year-old, he tells me of his plans.

When he delivers my son to me, we speak at the café, where I'd been writing all day, warmed by aspen burning in the woodstove, my cup brimming with fair trade, shade-grown coffee, my brain buzzing with pleasure. Comfort in the moment freezes immediately upon hearing his dream.

"When I was his age," he says, pointing his chin toward Elijah, who is already absorbed in the excitement of a brainteaser on-line, "it was already my goal to be a Marine."

Peacenik past aside, I am moved by his honesty and willingness to discuss his future with me, a former professor who offered to write him letters of recommendation for college in praise of his character. A terrific athlete, good student, smart and kind, he was, I thought, bound for the groves of Academe on scholarship ~ perhaps multiple scholarships. Around here, sports achievement, and football in particular, as in his case, often pays the fare to life outside our bucolic, patriotic village.

The conversation following his disclosure has me tiptoeing around several invisible boundary lines; he has not asked for advice, I remind myself, but I can't remain silent, as I did with the first grader, for whom war was at least a decade away. The babysitter's life will be in jeopardy within a year if he goes forward with this particular dream.

"There are many ways to serve your country," I say. He is by nature a helper, a teenager who volunteers with kids, the elderly, assists the members of his church in any way he can. If he were a Portlander, I might advise him to try Americorps, or, down the road, Peace Corps.

"My mother doesn't want me to go," he informs me, braces glinting in the sunlight. "She says she doesn't want me to die on the streets of Baghdad."

I tell him I don't want him to die there either, and if he were my son, I would tell him not to go. But he is not my son, though I worry about his life ~ his good heart and giving self. What do I advise? I want you to stay alive to serve, I tell him.

"What are your other interests?" I ask. "What were you thinking about majoring in at college?"

He tells me of his interest in physical therapy, perhaps sports medicine, which I see as the perfect segue into my go-to-college-first rap.

"Another way to serve your country would be to help veterans!" I suggest brightly. "You can get your degree, then work in an army hospital, helping soldiers who've returned with injuries."

As he shakes his head almost imperceptibly, I realize I've taken the wrong tack. That's a female approach, I tell myself, not macho enough, too like his mother's.

"My stepdad thinks it's a good idea," he says, looking at my son instead of me as Elijah plays math games, yahooing when he wins a game. "He's over in Iraq on his second tour. My stepdad's just National Guard, but I'd be a Marine, which is way better. Bunch of my friends are signing up too. "

The ides of March loom before us, with the war poised to enter its fifth year, death tolls escalating every month. Often, I overhear locals worrying about their family members in Iraq: siblings, children, in-laws, parents. A woman at the adjacent table informs her companion, "My nephew and uncle are leaving for their third tours." After several war years in Westcliffe, with its Fourth of July hoopla, and now Elijah's second babysitter contemplating boot camp, Iraq looms like a specter before me.

Raising my son, I emphasize negotiation of problems. I do not hit, though of course there are times I want to. "Use your words," I tell him, when he'd rather use his fists. Growing up, he has heard me growl at Bush's voice on the radio countless times. "You want to make war in Iraq," I shout at the boom box, "*You* go fight!" Other times I yell, "Send *your* daughters over there!" Bush Junior doesn't know anything about war, I tell my son; if Babs Jr. and Jenna were donning their Kevlar every morning to face IEDs, he would negotiate alternatives to bombs.

In World War II, my maternal uncle parachuted into enemy territory and was held prisoner by the Germans, suffering the rest of his life from what was then called shell shock. My surviving paternal cousins, Jews hiding in France and Rumania, survived in part due to American military might and lives. I am not a pacifist. Sometimes one must defend oneself or one's neighbor with whatever is at hand. But this is not one of those times.

This young, earnest man who is "big brother" to my son, an only child, tells me he needs to prove he's "got what it takes to become a man." Quickly, I cover my grimace at these words, which the babysitter believes in whole-heartedly, without irony.

"What does 'being a man' mean exactly, for you, at this point?" I ask, knowing I have to tone down or turn off any feminist language, or he won't hear me at all.

"Taking responsibility, serving my country, not running away from duty."

I nod. In his early life, which I know something about, his father deserted him and his sister as toddlers, leaving their mother, in her early twenties, to fend for their family.

When he's not in Iraq, the stepfather is a sheriff's deputy. Being a man is not an academic concept for this eighteen-year-old but rather a core issue in forming his identity, a nucleus around which he will make a life.

Back at the liberal arts college where I taught English for fifteen years, I used pinkies to make quotation marks around the word "manhood," as I dissected gender in literature. From *Beowulf* to Hemingway to Tim O'Brien, men continue to define themselves as warriors, inflicting violence instead of avoiding or repairing it.

"How will you be of use to the world as another casualty?" I ask.

He agrees that dead, he can serve no country, no cause, but he cannot nor is he willing to shake his fantasy of entering manhood as a Marine.

I can no longer afford quote marks. This sweet boy-man, whom my son adores, who earnestly wants to live, does not want me to talk him out of anything.

NITZA KOSHER PIZZA
1978

Elbow-deep in warm suds, pressed against the stainless steel sink, I feel my boss's muscular arms envelop me. "Quit it, Sam."

"Kisses sweet in wine, kisses sweet in wine," he says, kissing the back of my neck. Or is it "kisses sweet *and* wine?"

"Sam, leave me alone."

His wife, Marie, does the books in one of the booths while I scrub pots and bowls, the remainders of Sam's private time in the kitchen; no one is allowed while he prepares his "special sauce" for baked ziti.

A Yemenite Jew, Sam broke with his brother in biblical fashion and quit the family business in Flushing to start his own shop in Great Neck, a suburb with plenty of kosher Jews to patronize this dairy vegetarian restaurant, with falafel, tahini, and the best baked ziti on Long Island.

Sam wears heavy black shoes and the checked tweed trousers of a real chef, a starched cap cocked atop his head. By day's end, his apron is filthy.

Around Marie's pale neck hangs the star of David, a golden pendant also worn by her daughter, Teresa, 11 years old, who sits in another booth, doing homework. Last year, Marie converted to Judaism to marry Sam, who immigrated to New York as a teenager. He must be in his forties, Marie in her mid-thirties; I am 17.

"Why you don't like me kissing you? You need to laugh! To love! To feel joy! I make you feel joy," he says, kissing me over and over on the nape of my neck. He is short, just my height.

"Sam, your wife and daughter are ten feet away! Please leave me alone."

It's hard to push him away with real force, because his heavy arms feel so good, his backward embrace a kind of home.

"So what? She doesn't love me! And that girl isn't my daughter. Besides, Marie's not a beautiful Jewish girl like you, Anne." I've always hated my one-syllable name, but in his mouth, it sounds exotic.

His wife calls, and Sam backs off, storming through the swinging kitchen door, angry with her for interrupting his moment.

One of a handful of high school girls who work for Sam and Marie, I get minimum wage, under the table, plus tips. We work behind the counter and bring food from the kitchen. Sam tours the narrow aisle, booths on both sides, to schmooze with customers who love his food, which is, in fact, delicious.

My friends and I put up with Sam and his groping, which never goes beyond the hugs and kisses from behind. We think this is how it works in restaurants, as it has in every kitchen where I've washed dishes, including the Indian place by the train station and the pricey French bistro on the so-called Miracle Mile in Manhasset.

It's wrong to fool around with a married man, I tell myself, feeling virtuous about my ability to resist my boss's warm embrace. Sometimes, though, I *want* to turn from my suds and wrap myself around him, pressure him with my hips as hard as he presses me against the stainless steel sink. Sometimes I want his erection against me. It's not his looks, his manners, and certainly not his personality that keep me working there.

All fall, Rachel and I have been saving diligently for our trip across Canada and down California's coast after we graduate in January. When I started at Nitza Pizza last summer, Sam promised he would teach me how to make pizza, and I was thrilled ~ an actual skill to carry into my collegiate future! But when I burned my first pie, he ranted, swore, and prohibited me from learning more. I was banished to the kitchen, where I was more accessible than at the counter; his kisses sweet in wine moistened my neck again and again, me protesting, Sam ignoring my words.

High school ended, and the next day Rachel and I stepped onto the Amtrak "Montréaler" in Penn Station, future-bound. Although he had plenty of customers, Sam lost the shop the following summer, while Rachel and I were sleeping with brothers in Yosemite Valley. Reluctantly, he re-joined the family business in Queens, and Nitza Pizza ~ nitza meaning blossom or bud in Hebrew ~ receded into collective history, along with its celebrated ziti, baked by the Yemenite from Flushing with deft, loving hands.

ALMOST

1985

By that time, I'd broken almost every rule I would break. The smart girl from the "good" family," I'd slept with men of every race, creed and color. Most every drug had entered my lungs, my nose ~ though not my veins. I'd attempted suicide ~ "unsuccessfully" ~ more than once, and learned the art of trichotillomania, though I had no name at that time for such transgressions of the body. "You use yourself as an experiment," said my psychiatrist, years later. But he didn't know the depth and breadth of the experimentation preceding my arrival in his office.

"Almost," means just that, however. In my twenties, grad student by night, with a boring day job to pay the bills, the damage I had yet to do remained unfathomed. So when Victoria asked, "Want to try heroin," I thought she was kidding, because all I'd ever known her to do was drink. A sister-student in my Shakespeare class, we partied together on weekends, our entertainment consisting of binge drinking at bars, sometimes followed by crazy eating if we found ourselves without men by night's end. More than once, we concluded the party at Clown Alley at 2 in the morning, scarfing tuna melts with fries, smearing them into our hungry, gaping maws, so drunk and messy the owner threatened to kick us out.

Victoria was heavy, buxom, blond, innately savvy about how to catch and hold men's attention. She wore short black dresses with black heels, her shapely legs exposed. At the same time, she remained phenomenally insecure: born into a family of drunks, both terrified and certain she was heading the same way. By the time we met, she'd had three or four abortions, all of which she agonized over profoundly, all originating in drunken one-nighters with strangers, hoping for connection, love, affection ~ everything every one of us needs. Guilt over abortion drove her to the bottle, the pattern continuing.

I come from a family of crazy people, and we are crazy all on our own, without recourse to any genre of mind-altering substance, legal or otherwise.

69

We're Jews, not known for drinking as a culture, though of course Jewish drunks exist. We're just not known for it the way the Irish are ~ stereotype alert! ~ or Russians ~ second alert! ~ though these can be verified by personal anecdote. When I went to St. Petersburg, the smell of vodka permeated every hallway, and drunks of all ages staggered down the Nevsky Prospect, the city's equivalent of Fifth Avenue, in the sunshiny middle of the day. Though I drank, fish-like, with Victoria, I remembered reading in the poet John Berryman's unfinished memoir, *Recovery* (unfinished because he threw himself off a bridge in the frozen heart of a Minneapolis winter while composing it), "Jews don't drink." He hoped to make lots of Jewish friends in the asylum because he believed they never became alcoholics; perhaps he thought they were genetically incapable of it. I must have believed it too. In my family, my mother, my brother, myself were committed to psych wards without benefit of any substance at all.

I'd stayed away from drugs, especially hallucinogens. Even pot had been too much for me, propelling my brain to scary precipices of heightened realities: the congenial park down the street metamorphosed midday into a labyrinthine dark forest, the two blocks between my best friend's house and mine transformed themselves into the equivalent of an endless, terrorizing odyssey, rapists awaiting under every tree. I always told people, when they asked me to share a joint or drop acid, "My mind is a scary enough place all by itself, but thanks anyway."

"Heroin can't be compared to any other drug," Victoria insisted. We'd just snort it ~ nothing more. In fact, she said the high was softer and gentler than any drug I was talking about. A bit like the best drunk, only it didn't make you want to eat. In fact, you didn't think about food on heroin. For heavy women, this aspect held much appeal.

The night she introduced the idea of heroin to me, Victoria brought along her ex-boyfriend, conveniently accompanied by a friend for me as well, so there were four of us, neatly coupled. Her ex, Bill, now just a friend, had become a dealer, too deep in his habit to be sexual.

Evidently, I had done drugs before, so lawbreaking was not the ultimate transgression. Opiates held singular intrigue. It made sense that Victoria would be attracted to heroin, alone among other drugs, for it shed an otherworldly light, not associated in her mind with junkies on Mission Street, but literati in London's fin-de-siècle opium dens, formally dressed for their dreamy reach into oblivion.

Did I say no? I did not. I was curious. If she had suggested using needles, my refusal would have been automatic. But snorting? What harm could that do?

Bill brought it along to our meeting at the Savoy Café in North Beach. Each of us had to pay a certain sum of money ~ I no longer remember what it was ~ no more than twenty bucks. Stan, his friend, was broke after our first glass of wine, so I ended up paying for "my date" and me to drink several rounds.

Victoria had done heroin before, exactly in this way, though Bill had advanced to the needle. After hours at the Savoy, drinking some sort of red wine I no longer drink, Bill said we should go out back. The rain had cleared, and one could see stars in the San Francisco sky ~ not a common occurrence. I sat on a damp curb, waiting passively for the event to unfold, a spectator at my own life.

Stan unfolded a rectangle of aluminum foil, Bill provided the heroin and the lighter, and we began. The longer we sat there, the brighter the constellations glowed. Doubtless my ass was damp and stiff from the wet cement, but I remember none of those details. Apparently, it never crossed my mind that we could get caught, sitting on the curb snorting our opiate. I remember laughing, though, delighted by whatever delights one in a drunken state, Victoria and I all over giggles, while the men remained quiet.

Did we laugh because we felt such well-being? Perhaps. I only managed a few snorts before I said I'd had enough. "More for me," said Stan. He was bland, a man whose sole outstanding descriptor was that he was a gardener at a golf course, and had to be on the greens at 6 a.m. the next day. I didn't care about him. Would I spend the night with him? I didn't think about it. The moments there on the curb, observing the stars where they didn't usually exist, constituted an isolated envelope of bliss. At once, I understood the allure of the drug: the idea that one needed nothing else in the world.

Victoria never told me how sick I would get.

A purposeful evasion, a convenient elision of truth? That night, at the gardener's studio apartment, I woke in the darkness and needed to vomit, but I didn't know where I was or who he was or where a bathroom might be. He was yelling some sort of direction to a toilet, but I couldn't understand his words. I threw up on the floor, the carpet, and finally in the kitchen sink. Stan was pissed. At 5, when the alarm went off, he told me I had to leave the apartment; a key was required to lock the door, and he had no extra. Somehow, I called for a taxi, still dry-heaving, my brain now recoiling from what I had done to it.

The cab driver surveyed me, assessed the damage, and said nothing all the way to my apartment, me with my head out the window in case I got sick again. It took days to recover, my head ringing with pain, whoever I was more disordered and directionless than ever before.

Was that night the nadir of my existence? Drunk, stoned on heroin, in bed with a stranger ~ I have no idea if we had sex, but I didn't get pregnant or any STDs that night ~ and puking all over the floor? How deeply I descended in that man's apartment, my body beyond my control, my soul atomized by copious amounts of alcohol with heroin as the flourish on top. "These fragments I have shored against my ruins," wrote Eliot in *The Wasteland*. Slowly, I began to gather my fragments, harvesting bits of self, scattered like meteorites everywhere.

RESCUED AND HUMBLE
2006

Amazingly, I live here, along with my son, two rescue dogs, countless antelope and a host of diverse people from all manner of backgrounds, a community somehow ~ by luck at birth or greater luck at homing in on this Valley later in life ~ cohabiting peacefully under skies huge with billowing cumulus and autumn aspens fluttering golden beneath the blue.

At the local coffee shop, a grizzled, tattooed biker regales the retired literature professor with tales of his daughter's wedding to an Orthodox Jew back East. A rancher just returned from Argentina discusses our new radio station with the fine-arts photographer who engineers the station. Painters, plumbers, teachers, and realtors exchange news of family, complain about the price of gas and adore the weather over straight-up coffee, lattés and white chocolate mochas before heading to work each morning.

On Main Street, children leave their bikes unattended while checking out books at the expanded local library, where the free-for-donation shelves sport offerings as varied as French-to-Spanish dictionaries, Nancy Drew mysteries, *Introduction to Geology*, *The Definitive Crockpot Cooking Bible* and home-schooling curricula, secular and Christian. On the take-an-issue, leave-an-issue magazine racks, one can find *Tennis Monthly*, *The London Review of Books*, *Sunset Magazine*, *The Economist*, *Western Homes*, and *Ode*, among other offerings.

Every Thursday, the weekly newspaper is consumed cover-to-cover for the local skinny as well as Valley connections to the larger world. A local young woman and her Tibetan husband send bulletins on the recent earthquake in China, soliciting donations from Sichuan province. We learn of inevitable vehicular encounters with deer, current population of the county jail (the *Tribune* calls it the "hoosegow") ~ generally a handful of men, 1 woman ~ the time and place of spaghetti fundraising dinners to help residents with no insurance and too many medical bills, openings of new shows at the Third Street Gallery, obituaries of current and former residents, births of grandchildren local and distant, military and academic achievements of recent grads of Custer County High, and, of course, the classifieds, in which one can buy anything from a cutting-edge snowplow to laying hens to widescreen HDTV to "ugly old Jimmy panel truck, but works."

In this valley, we look after each other. Last winter, after my car got high-centered in serious snow, my son, dogs and I hiked back a mile in ten-degree weather to a neighbor, who drove us to the top of our driveway, fearing the same fate. In our snow boots, we trudged through knee-deep mounds back to where our adventure started. Just as we were planning a day by necessity to be spent at home, I heard an unfamiliar noise: a horn, right in front of my snowed-in cabin! It was my boss's husband, driving his snowplow. Although my phone didn't work, my boss had intuited we were stuck and sent him to rescue us.

Some days, that's how it feels to live here: to be rescued. Nature offers succor, neighbors offer help, and though the world and its vicissitudes never cease their daily rounds, we remain humble yet strong in this, our beloved landscape.

THE YUCK FACTOR
2008

One friend called it the "yuck factor."

My mother said resolutely, "You just can't understand it."

When I tried to persuade her that one could *try* ~ that that's what I'd been doing with my novel for the last four years ~ she couldn't grasp that understanding is possible.

After reviewing the 1981 NPR "Father Cares" program, based on the radio play by James Reston Jr., author of *Our Father, Who Art in Hell* and reporter Noah Adams, I revisit the fact that the public face of Jonestown belongs to Jim Jones, and the face portrayed is always that of a madman.

My novel, *Paradise Undone,* is not about Jim Jones.

The "great man" theory of history tires and bores me. My task as a writer is to unveil the faces of the women and men beside the endlessly repeated name and outsized ego of the leader. I wrote the book to expose their lives and voices, to give some "airtime" to a few of the other 917 people who died on November 18, 1978, though nearly 30 years later, it remains Jim-Jones-the-Madman as litany, as explanation, as the whole story.

As I write this essay, *Paradise Undone* is being read by a number of editors at a handful of publishers in New York. So far, approximately 24 big East Coast presses have turned it down for various reasons, some of them having to do with subject matter, some with style, some with lack of ability to "sell" the novel or even the idea of the novel to colleagues, and thus to the public.

When I listen to those voices on the tapes, it is not Jim Jones I want to know more about. Frankly, I would prefer to hear less of him. I want to know about the older black woman who says so earnestly, "You're the only father I have. You're the only family I have. I gave up my brother for you."

On the highly selective NPR program, Jones turns the moment into a self-serving commercial: sing your song, he tells the woman. So she sings "I Never

Heard a Man Speak Like This Man Before." Everyone sings along, but Jones's voice is loudest. I'd rather hear her tell her story instead.

"Why did you leave your brother to follow Jim Jones?" I would ask her. "Tell me how you came to Peoples Temple."

In the FBI documents, I have located some of these old women's stories and incorporated them into my novel. But their voices have receded from public memory, like so many of those standing in the shadows cast by Jones and other cult leaders.

My friend George tried to prepare me for the rejections. "It's not your writing that they'll be reacting to," he told me very kindly. "They'll be imagining all those bloated bodies on TV and saying to themselves, 'Yuck! Who wants to read about that?'"

Whether or not my continued applications to editors prove George right, I plan to keep writing. The next book is percolating.

LES INVISIBLES AT THE DINNER TABLE
2009

Around the dinner table, friends recount their travels to family manses in the Old Country. Anita describes the house in Spain that's been home to generations of her mother's family, brimming with relatives eating three-hour meals under the arbor. Her grandmother immigrated to the New World of the Caribbean, and her parents to the United States when she was a child. We thrill to her descriptions of the centuries-old dwelling of stone, its architecture in harmony with its desert-like surroundings, not unlike the house in which we enjoy her spicy Cuban beans, with its wide archways and unfettered Sangre de Cristo views.

Gretchen tells of her grandmother's home in Austria, where at 99 she still presides over multiple generations who have made that valley home for centuries. Her own mother left for Canada, then the United States, needing independence from all those relatives, but Gretchen is wistful as she speaks of extended family all in one place, where their dead have always been buried.

As others talk, I ponder my own familial history in Europe: my Jewish forebears did not retain their ancestral homes. Russian ancestors huddled inside darkened rooms while Cossacks rode on Good Friday rampages, breaking windows in Jewish homes and worse.

On his father's side, my son descends from Congolese brutalized by French slavers on their enforced journey to the island of Saint-Domingue, which became Haiti in the first successful slave revolt of the New World. Likewise, his father's people have no home in the "Old Country," no dwelling to mark their earliest existence because those in control of their destinies deemed them less than human.

When Anita recalls the beauty of Spain, I remember my own trip to Toledo, where I got spooked visiting a medieval synagogue, devoid of Jews since the Inquisition, despite the sign: "Toledo was home to a lively Jewish population of ten thousand." Five centuries before the Holocaust, this corner of the Old World emptied itself of Jews; those on the Iberian Peninsula might convert to Catholicism instead of die.

At the home of El Greco, a guard singled me out. "*Judia?*" he asked. Why did he want to know? Would I be penalized ~ perhaps run out of town ~ if I answered in the affirmative? I nod. My Jewishness is written on my face. He points to his nose. "I thought so," he tells me in Spanish. "*La nariz.*"

To that Spaniard, my identity was marked upon my person, as my son is marked by the color of his skin, making us unlike the others at this party, where, in 2009 we eat and drink, laughing and talking politics while I wonder about the people who no longer reside here: descendants of indigenous people who first populated this valley, and the offspring of black cowboys who drove cattle through these mountain passes ~ their invisible presences. In Haiti, they are called *les invisibles*, the spirits of the dead who are with us, always, whether we honor them or not.

DOME LIFE
1979

Imagine a transparent dome atop Bennett's and Julia's pot farm in Mendocino County. Clear and permeable walls, so one can pass inside and out without anyone noticing. To the eye, no discernible difference exists between interior and exterior. Inside, however, the air bristles with paranoia, redolent with freshly cut marijuana: harvest time.

We'd come for a week's visit, our goal to decide whether we should accept our friends' offer: free rent, wild land and sky and open terrain, a view stretching to the coastal range, living in our converted yellow 1951 GMC schoolbus beside their converted custom painted blue-and-white Chevy one, far from city life and its rules. We would need to stay put only during growing season, our presence a deterrent to thieves, so that Bennett and Julia could leave to do business and the other things one did out in the real world.

Coyotes, deer, eagles and hawks, cumulonimbus blossoming up and west, unencumbered by anything manufactured. It was a magical place, with shelter from the elements in a copse of manzanita. Their bus was parked a half-mile from the rarely traveled road up the mountain ~ only a few dozen dropouts lived up here off the grid. Some had sheep, others cattle. One family was trying to start an apple orchard. There were trust-fund babies, like Julia, who wanted to read and paint and make art, along with old street-smart types, like Bennett, who'd done every kind of job in their lives, legal and otherwise, to make a buck.

Outside the dome, where I'd lived until then, was a place of laws and rules and the structures of daily life. My boyfriend painted houses while I took college classes, working behind the counter in a Mexican restaurant on weekends. For years, his boss in the painting business had been Bennett, until he and Julia drove up that mountain road two growing seasons earlier to try another life, one free of social security numbers and time clocks and neighbors. We'd visited before, but never at harvest.

On earlier trips, we didn't see any dome, as it descended only at reaping time. In that era, "medical marijuana" had not yet taken root. Bennett and Julia grew dope because money was to be made illegally, untaxed, unmarked, in great quantities ~ *if* you were disciplined. Before they moved, our friends told stories about foolish growers they'd met, men and women whose profits "flew up their noses," when savvy city dealers arrived not with cash but cocaine. The trade of one drug for another triggered days or weeks of partying, after which remained no cash for the rest of the year ~ nothing left to pay for diapers, food, car repairs, fuel. One still needs money, even up there. Though Julia had no children with Bennett, many other farmers were fertile and reproduced often, the pregnant women fragrant with THC as they worked in the fields or drying sheds, clipping and trimming with their grandmothers' seam-rippers borrowed from another era of handmade clothes on Midwestern farms raising corn and alfalfa.

I was 19: part of me wanted to be like Julia, a Boston sophisticate who'd fled her parents' uptight, upper class ways and means to become an outlaw. Or I might model myself after the hippie farmers we met at the market in town: make babies and homemade preserves, my little one snug in a sling while I worked the land.

David was five years older but still impressionable, a high school egghead who, once introduced to drugs, metamorphosed into a pleasure seeker. Horribly shy, he wore thick glasses; I was his first girlfriend. Vulnerable to charismatic Bennett's persuasion, he envisioned an easy natural life. Why not move up there? We wouldn't do anything illegal ourselves. David wasn't in love with painting houses, nor I with my restaurant job and general education classes. He'd already asked me to marry him ~ David's dreams were entwined with hippie women and babies, the route his big brother had taken ~ but I wasn't quite ready. Let's just live together, see how it feels, I told him.

We hadn't foreseen Yanana getting murdered. A friend of Julia's, she lived in a real geodesic dome down the mountain, traded her crop for money (or so we thought) from San Francisco dealers. No one ever discovered what happened. That Sunday, a neighbor dropping by to bring her fresh eggs walked in on a crime scene: Yanana's body slashed to pieces, the place ripped inside out from loft to the dirt beneath the deck, where she'd buried her grandmother's trunk. Even her compost container lay dumped on the floor, coffee grounds and eggshells scattered around and atop her body. Who knows what they were looking for, and what they found, if anything?

Yanana's real name was Deirdre O'Sullivan, one of the *éminences grises* in the community. In 1962, she'd been a straight-arrow salesgirl at Macy's, an Irish Catholic schoolgirl graduated from Immaculate Conception Academy, daughter of a muckety-muck in San Francisco politics. She'd grown up in the lace-curtain Castro district, before it became renowned for men in tiny shorts kissing on street corners. Her childhood left her straitlaced and pure, marrying the boy next door, both of them virgins, planning a life to parallel their parents'. Then came the Summer of Love.

The sheriff did little more than a cursory investigation ~ dead growers were no longer news. That afternoon, we drove by her dome but did not leave the road, though plenty of townspeople congregated around Yanana's home, like vultures on carrion, looking for.... Drugs? Money? Guns? Whatever the killer/thieves had failed to find, perhaps.

During our beer run to town, which included the weekly post office pick-up for Bennett and Julia ~ no bills in their mail ~ a dealer from L.A. had come and gone at the bus.

When we returned, Julia was sitting on Bennett's lap, her finger in his mouth, rubbing his gums. He was doing the same to her. "Over there, on the counter," said Julia, her grin so wide it exposed the flesh above her teeth.

On a Scrabble board-size mirror lay a spiral of white powder with a scissored-down drinking straw at the outer edge, like a maze in a child's magazine. Start here, at the arrow in red. Where did one exit? The end wasn't marked.

"Go on! It's a present from our Los Angeles friend."

Bennett and Julia were so jolly already we had much to do to catch up. That spiral made me nervous. It just sat there, compliantly, waiting to be snorted. By whom? How often? For how long?

"Is this all your profit, right here?" I asked, pointing to the mirror after I took a tiny, tentative toot, just to show I was no chicken.

Grandly, Bennett waved toward the sky. "Hell no! There's plenty more where that came from. Go on! David, get her a real snootful this time!"

We looked at one another, unsure. A few times, we'd used cocaine as a communication aid; awkward and unlike, we often didn't know how to talk to one another. With coke, reticence evaporated. We chatted easily, laughing, planning our future together. On those occasions, we stayed up all night fooling around, but for me, our conversation was the best part. David was so quiet; sometimes, when I asked him what he was thinking, he would bark, "I'm not thinking anything! You're always trying to drag words out of me!" Undaunted, I believed he was hiding a world of lively ideas inside his calm demeanor. When we were high together, his garrulousness proved me right.

David guided my head down, holding the straw for me, so I inhaled. All day, all night, we descended the spiral, watched it shrink into nothing. Around dawn, after no sleep and much animated, forgettable talk among the four of us, I wanted more cocaine. It was all gone. The intensity of my desire made me understand I had now passed by osmosis inside the dome. Had David come through beside me? I couldn't tell.

We came from different worlds, like Bennett and Julia.

Inside the dome, people carried shotguns; cocaine and murder coincided. With difficulty, I stepped down from the bus into fresh autumn air, beckoning David to follow. At the mirror, he and Bennett were trailing wet fingertips across the glass, taking turns licking it.

"David, we have to get out of here."

"I know."

Thirty minutes later, we were speeding down the mountain, fleeing the dome and its toxicity. That day, we both felt lucky to have escaped with our lives. Eventually, David would return to it, alone, and lose his teeth to meth. He might survive inside the dome, but I never allowed myself to approach such dangerous transparency again.

JONESTOWN, A "HARD SELL"
2020

The 30-year anniversary of Jonestown came and went without my four protagonists having their say. Five years into my obsession with writing a novel about Jonestown, the book had gone through multiple drafts and titles: *Fathom These Events*; *Jonestown Perfume*; *Resurrection City*; and, finally, *Paradise Undone: A Novel of Jonestown*.

It had an agent for a while, and was under close consideration by a major publishing company, only to be rejected because the sales staff wasn't "on the same page" with the editor, who said he really liked it, but he was new to the company and didn't want to "force the book down their throats," he informed me, in an ill-chosen Kool-Aid-esque locution. The book might have interested another major firm, but that publisher was already contracted for a non-fiction book about Jonestown, and didn't want to handle two books simultaneously on the same subject.

A very small press accepted *Paradise Undone* but that deal ran into trouble, and a few months later came undone. The collapse may or may not have been precipitated by my versions of Jim and Marceline Jones, and the fictionalized characters of Truth Miller, a Peoples Temple member who remained in the Bay Area, Virgil Nascimento, a Guyanese ambassador to the United States, and Watts Freeman, a composite based on the young men who escaped from Jonestown on November 18th, 1978. Later, I would learn that the publisher was bipolar, and his descent into unreason ~ which prompted my departure from the press ~ was due to his withdrawal from medication.

One section of the novel, "*I* Will Never Let You Down," was a finalist in *Glimmer Train Stories'* "Family Matters" contest. Yet another, "Knowing What I Know," was published in *Driftwood: A Literary Journal of Voices from Afar* (2006), and sent me to a writer's workshop in southern France on a partial scholarship. Two sections of the book appeared online: in *Joyland* ("Jonestown, Japantown,") and *Fictive Dream* ("Long Before Jonestown"). Most promisingly, the first chapter of my book was a semi-finalist in the inaugural Amazon Breakthrough Novel Contest, receiving nearly 50 super-positive reader reviews ~ some of them written by complete strangers! But about 40 publishers reached through my agent said no. All of them said Jonestown is a "hard sell." Maybe it's the subject, or my treatment of it, or possibly ~ probably ~ both that have made *Paradise Undone: A Novel of Jonestown* so difficult to offer to the world in book form in order that readers might experience for themselves my idiosyncratic version of the rise and fall of Peoples Temple as well as the aftermath of Jonestown.

Fortunately, artists keep making art about Peoples Temple, scholars keep studying, and survivors keep telling their stories. Each year now, documentaries and plays, operas and memoirs, academic articles, scholarly volumes and visual art emerge to inform those who know about Jonestown and those who are only now learning of this powerful, profound moment in 20th century American history.

By 2020, without an agent, my book had made finalist in 14 competitions, and been rejected 279 times, complete with a new epilogue to acknowledge the 40th anniversary of the massacre in 2018.

Whether "hard sell" or no, the truth will out ~ sooner or later.

TEETH
2010

Somewhere in the cerebral folds of memory, doubtless, the accident exists. Twenty-five years later, after many thousands of dollars to dentists, prosthodontists, oral surgeons, not to mention the shrinks, therapists, psychopharmacologists, only fragments linger, like the shards of light spoken of in the Kabbalah, waiting to be reassembled and restored to god. Few whole pieces remain: flat on my back in a pick-up bed beside the borrowed too-large 10 speed, the Adirondack stars scintillating overhead in their unmoved constellations; humans blurring around the truck parked beside the Teardrop in front of the Main House; no one was allowed to see me in my condition ~ what was it? ~ during the hour-long wait for the ambulance; this was deep North Country, the closest hospital 60 miles away. Later, or the next day, the whiteness of the hospital, elbows, knees and jaw crazy-quilt stitched into place, the missing teeth. I learned a new word when I read the reports, years later: buccogingival, mouth and gum in Latin.

Forward a dozen years to my favorite Indian restaurant in Portland, Oregon, where friends and I were munching our samosas when a tray passed on a waiter's arm, heaped with sizzling Biryani rice. Something about the size of the grains, their bloody appearance in the sauce, such a dislocated vision made me say to a friend, "Look at the ... teeth!" I could not locate "r-i-c-e" in my brain, the sight of Biryani having jarred some enamel shards from memory, resting on a sterile silver salver.

Last week, I bought an outrageously expensive vacuum from a straggly-haired traveling salesman, payable by installment over three years. The vacuum I owned worked fine, but he was missing teeth. Two right up front, which I'd just had replaced, again, for the third time since the accident.

Shortly after my sojourn in Saranac Lake Hospital, I returned to my home in San Francisco, where I would continue my graduate studies come September. I remember walking to the oral surgeon for the first of many appointments to replace the previously orthodontically perfect set of teeth in my mouth with something serviceable. I lived in the Mission District, on Guerrero Street, where I shared the streets with many poor and homeless. On Mission Street, waiting for the bus, I observed how very many poor people, often Hispanic or African-American but white as well, all these poor individuals in the heart of prosperous America, had few teeth, bad teeth, or no teeth.

When I crashed, I was dead drunk. Not dead, but as drunk as you could be from alcohol poisoning and still breathing. That day, I wanted to die.

A father of a girl on my son's soccer team is missing a front tooth. Everywhere I see him ~ at the supermarket or on the sidelines of the soccer field ~ I see the gap, the lacuna in his mouth, advertising his poverty. Often, at my store-sightings, he is dressed in painting whites, a tough profession around here, with lots of competition and few jobs to bid. Self-employed, the first thing to go is health insurance, and don't even think about dental.

When a friend asked how much my implants would cost, I swallowed and said, "Twelve thousand dollars."

"That's not too bad," she replied, and I nearly choked on my veggie burger.

"You don't think twelve thousand dollars is a lot of money?!"

Now, it was her turn to choke. "I thought you said twelve hundred dollars!" She said all this in her lovely New Zealand accent, which somehow made the "thousand" sound like even more money, like a million bucks.

During his long years of workaholism, my father made a lot of money. He wasn't around much, and when he was, he was almost always exhausted. My first book was about a family wherein the father deserts his family on the first page. It was pure fiction, about an invented family quite unlike my own. Or so I thought. When my publisher accepted the book, he asked, "Did your father desert your family? It's so realistic!"

Truthfully, I said no. My father came home every night. Never an affair, not even any friends, really. Just work and sleep. An immigrant. A double immigrant, fleeing the Nazis for China, then fleeing the Communists for here, where, eventually, he became a rich man. A man able to pay for his daughter's endless teeth replacements.

A prudent man, he left everything to my mother, who never spends money. So now, even after my father's death a decade ago, he is still paying for my teeth.

My guess is that the housepainter single father with the gap does not have a wealthy widow for a mother, one who will pay for her children's teeth problems. Simultaneously, this fall, my sister, my brother and I all needed bridge replacements, and all of us are unemployed. All of us, in California, Colorado and New York, are providing prosthodontists, oral surgeons and various dentist-types with second homes, or at least trips to Barcelona, like my prosthodontist took in the midst of my six-month procedure.

***

A young girl had come to the door, offering a free rug shampoo if I agreed to listen to the vacuum-seller's spiel. I thought she was selling the vacuums, but after an absence of 15 minutes, the stringy-haired Frank arrived with all his props in tow.

Except front teeth.

His very long presentation ~ comparing his stainless steel Kirby to my used plastic model I'd purchased from the vacuum repair guy who couldn't fix my old one ~ was polished and impressive. Surely, who wouldn't want such a stellar machine, with its Art Deco looks and ability to clean Venetian blinds and spray paint in addition to ordinary carpet cleaning?

In the course of his patter, he let drop that he was a single father, having raised two sons to responsible manhood, though one had recently died in a car accident. During his demo, he asked my son to help, garnering Elijah's appreciation as well as his admiration for the high tech, automobile-like Kirby Special. It's hard to be a single parent, he said, correctly assessing the shape of my family, the two dogs put in the yard so as not to bark at the mechanical din.

My son, who is ten, with lovely teeth all around, kept whispering to me, "You don't have to buy this, Mom." Elijah knew the salesman had me, but he did not know why. Frank told us about the trip that the sales force was competing for, a vacation somewhere in Oklahoma. He said he hadn't had a vacation in nearly 18 years, as his boys and their needs had always taken priority. If I bought a vacuum from him, he would be closer to his sales goal, one step toward that Oklahoma rest.

"Mom, you really don't need to buy this vacuum," Elijah told me again.

"I know, honey, but it's a good investment. It's not very much for a forever guaranty on a machine I'll use for the rest of my life, right?" I'm 50, and say I live another 30 or more years, a few thousand bucks amortizes into just pennies per day, or something like that. Elijah couldn't argue with the math, and I was on my third plastic vacuum in three years already.

If Frank had been selling encyclopedias ~ do they still sell them door to door? ~ would I have bought a set? Given the teeth factor, probably. I could make a pretty good argument for a sturdy Encyclopedia Britannica, despite the ever-present Internet.

I don't often think about my teeth these days, except for moments when I need to rip open a bag of chips, and the prosthodontist's warning comes back to me: "Don't use these teeth to open anything!" And then I search for scissors or a knife.

The housepainter's daughter stopped playing soccer, so I rarely see him anymore, and haven't bumped into him at the supermarket lately. The lady who used to clean my son's pre-school, missing even more teeth than the housepainter, she hasn't been around either.

Last month, I celebrated my 50th birthday with old friends at that same Indian restaurant. We ordered no Biryani, but my friend remembered that moment long ago, calling out, "Look at the teeth!" as a steaming platter sailed by on the waiter's shoulder, the moment when teeth and food and life melded into sustenance.

A LONG AND SUFFERING PEOPLE
2008

"I am quite capable of organizing the suicide aspect + will follow through
+ try to convey concern + warmth
throughout the ordeal."

~ Dr. Larry Schacht, in a letter to Jim Jones in Guyana, 1978

The doctor who masterminded the cyanide poisoning at Jonestown was Jewish.

The mandate to Jews in the Kabala is *tikkun olam*, "To heal and repair the world." Before attending medical school, Larry Schacht wrote to Jim Jones that he hoped "to fulfill my goal to be of service to suffering humanity in the medical profession." Dr. Schacht strayed so far from this mandate as to become the embodiment of all that stands opposed to this fundamental tenet of Judaism.

Robert Jay Lifton, himself a Jewish doctor, examined the paradox of doctors who harm instead of heal in *The Nazi Doctors: Medical Killing and the Psychology of Genocide* (1988). Lifton observed how, once given the opportunity, men of medicine ~ and the Nazi doctors he interviewed were exclusively male ~ moved easily from maintaining to violating their Hippocratic oath. As Hitler encouraged the use of human beings ~ primarily Jewish and Roma ~ for medical experiments, many doctors were eager to comply, often masking their sadism in the guise of advancing medical knowledge.

Schacht had no such guile. In his recent article, "Jonestown's Medicine Man," Craig Malisow of *The Houston Press*, writes, "'Undetermined' might be an apt descriptor for how Schacht, a middle-class, well-educated Jewish man from Houston, wound up in a secluded jungle compound, researching the most effective ways to slaughter men, women and children, in the first place."

Also unlike the Nazi doctors discussed in Lifton's disturbing book, Schacht went to his death along with his "subjects." His body, like so many of the others, had deteriorated in Guyana's intense tropical heat long before a meaningful autopsy could be performed a few weeks later in Delaware. The coroner's conclusion, "undetermined," failed to prove definitively that Schacht had indeed tasted his own medicine. The two who died by gunshot ~ Jim Jones and Annie Moore ~ clearly were not victims of the poisoned brew. By force or by choice, 907 human beings ingested Schacht's lethal concoction on November 18, 1978, and it is probable he was one of the last to do so. As he had written earlier that year, it was likely he was there to "try to convey concern + warmth throughout the ordeal," as he used a stethoscope to confirm death. The coldness of that façade of care mirrors his predecessors in the Nazi death camps.

By 1978, the details of the Holocaust were widely known. Not a child of survivors, like the Tropp siblings, Schacht apparently made no connections between the mass murders perpetrated by the *einsatzgruppen* and in the gas chambers of the extermination camps, with the mass murders of Jonestown. Thirty-three years after the liberation of Dachau, a Jewish doctor and his "research" caused the deaths of primarily African-American men, women and children, along with other whites, Jews, and Native Americans in the largest mass death of American civilians in the twentieth century.

* * *

On the last day of Jonestown, Dick Tropp, one of the community's chroniclers, wrote:

> As I write these words, people are silently amassed, taking a quick
> potion, inducing sleep, relief. We are a long and suffering people. I
> wish I had time to put it all together ~ the meaning of a people ~ a
> struggle, to find the symbolic and eternal in this moment ~ I wish
> that I had done it. I did not do it. I failed.

Dick's sister, Harriet, a P.R. person for Jones and Peoples Temple, summoned the memory of the Warsaw Ghetto fighters when she compared the beleaguered ~ or so she believed ~ Jonestown members to those Jewish rebels who died trying to escape the fate the surrounding Nazi's intended for them.

"This has been the unanimous vote of the collective community here in Guyana," she told the world in a radio broadcast the previous spring as the leaders of Jonestown protested what they perceived was harassment of community residents by relatives and government agencies back in the United States. "We choose as our model, not those who marched submissively into gas ovens, but the valiant heroes who resisted in the Warsaw Ghetto."

* * *

Sharon Amos, also Jewish, was the sole Temple member not living in Jonestown to obey the call to suicide. Though she was working for the Temple in Guyana's capital of Georgetown with her three children, her spirit was with the mass murder occurring miles away; she killed her two daughters and son before committing suicide. Not with poison, but a knife.

How did so many Jews fail to heed the Santayana quote posted above Jim Jones's "throne" in Jonestown's central gathering place, around which were heaped so many bodies? This photograph has become an iconic testament to our human failure to learn from the evils perpetrated in our collective history.

"Those who do not remember the past are condemned to repeat it." Jorge Agustín Nicolás Ruiz de Santayana y Borrás, known as George Santayana (d. 1952), penned those words in 1905, before the litany of horrors of the twentieth century began.

The "long and suffering people" to whom Schacht, the Tropps and Amos belonged ~ Jews ~ were familiar with such horrors long before World War I, the first attempted genocide of the century of the Armenians by the Turks, and all the monstrosities of the 1900s which followed...

And yet...

No one learns from history. No one.

EXTRATEMPORAL
2014

For six days and nights, he remained immobile, pinned between the decomposing body of his older friend, behind the steering wheel, and the passenger door, which had smashed into the rocky terrain. Six months later, Kenny remembered nothing, though others reconstructed the story from available details. No seat belts on either man as they drove, vaguely drunk, home from the city to their rented house in a depressed rural Colorado town. Fortunately, the October night chill kept Richard's body from swelling and stinking, yet it ensured Kenny's future as an amputee: frostbite took both feet and three fingers on his left hand.

I also live in that economically struggling hamlet, where I read about the accident in our local paper, a week after it occurred, amazed that the younger man, who was in his 40s ~ younger than me ~ could have survived such an ordeal. Kenny's father told the reporter that his son's survival was "a miracle, absolutely." He repeated how grateful they were, he and the rest of Kenny's family, but the article didn't specify to whom.

Some have faith, some religion, others spirituality. Me, I can understand Kenny's father's gratitude: sometimes, waking in the dark dawn to the mourning doves cooing outside my window is enough to make an atheist bow her head in thanks.

Both Kenny and Richard were drunks, often unemployed, usually delinquent on child support payments to former wives: two in Richard's case, only one for Kenny. Their children, who lived in Denver and elsewhere, ranging from 14 to 34, rarely saw or communicated with their fathers. "Deadbeat Dads" is the term politicians use to describe these two ~ men sinking into their own morass, sometimes fast, more often with excruciating slowness.

On a good day, Kenny could repair engines with the best mechanics in Denver. Hungover and/or drunk, he was still superior to 90% of the capital's car repair professionals. When there was extra work to be had, garage owners summoned Kenny from the boonies. He and Richard would drive in for a few days, or as long as the work lasted, staying in motels, eating fast food, drinking.

Though I've lived here a decade, I never knew Kenny or Richard, though I am acquainted with Kenny's dad, who runs the garage with the best local reputation. Frankly, I was surprised when the newspaper pinpointed the familial connection, because Kenny's dad doesn't look old enough to have a son 43 years old, much less a total disaster of an adult. Fit and sober, Kenny's dad prides himself on excellent service and low prices for the poorest in our community ~ he's let customers pay in firewood, or fresh eggs, or a series of extremely low payments that might outlast the old man or woman to whom he'd been kind.

When they weren't out drinking, the two men stayed home and watched a lot of TV, the blue glow escaping their windows to illuminate the dirt road on which they lived. Town gossips speculated on what these two men might really be doing, keeping house together in a tiny one-bedroom old miner's cabin. Long ago, our village was one of those spectacular mining successes, with an opera house and multiple overnight millionaires. But that magnanimous story was born and bred of a prior century. The magnates' mansions have been torn down or divided into decaying apartments. Of the small cabins dotting the hills, old tailings in the backyards of some, many had been home to a miner who mailed his riches back to distant wives and children. These poorly insulated tiny homes are now dwellings for the poorest citizens, the mines long depleted of their valuable ore. In the 21st century, "white trash" is what cruel people call Coloradans like Kenny and Richard.

Without delay, Kenny's legs were amputated below the knees. He has a rod in his right thigh, plates in his jaw, pins in his left elbow. As he has no regular job, Kenny is without insurance, so his father has thrown multiple fundraising spaghetti dinners to pay the bills.

My own accident was far less dramatic, nearly thirty years back, but reading about Kenny and his lost days in the car reminded me of my own mysteriously lapsed time, which lasted a few hours, perhaps ~ at any rate, less than one night. Like Richard, I was also a drunk driver, but of a bicycle instead of a car. Unlike them, I was alone.

Habitually, Richard and Kenny would drive back from Denver in the early morning hours to avoid traffic, and, more to the point, to steer clear of sheriffs. Both had DUI histories, and suspended licenses at one time or other. When the accident happened, Kenny's license had been pulled for 8 months of a yearlong suspension; hence, Richard drove. Bottles of beer, empty and full, were found in the wreck, and though by the time the men were discovered ~ too late to test their blood alcohol ~ it would have been typical for both to drink while driving. Ultimately, whether Richard was drunk or sober behind the wheel makes no difference. Although they'd taken the same route hundreds, perhaps thousands of times, they managed a peculiar feat: somehow, at the northernmost curve of the serpentine highway, the car jumped the guardrail and catapulted down to the valley floor, perhaps a distance of 30 feet. According to the authorities, Richard died on impact.

Because they didn't crash *into* the guardrail, breaking it in two, as others had before them, and since the wreck had wedged itself beneath scrub oaks in the shadow of the highway stanchions, their time capsule/coffin could not be seen by drivers from either direction.

At first, their absence was not remarkable. Richard and Kenny were taking a few extra days to work in the city. Or, they had begun a major bender. Both scenarios had occurred in the past, so the fact that the men hadn't returned didn't immediately bother Kenny's dad, who would speak with his son once a week on average. Often, Kenny would stop by the shop for a cup of bitter coffee, chatting with the guys in the garage, catching up with his father on the doings of his four siblings, numerous nieces and nephews.

No missing persons report was ever filed. By the sixth day, however, Kenny's dad began to worry. In the past, under similar circumstances, Kenny would telephone ~ just to report his whereabouts. Since his last year in high school, Kenny's drinking had led to innumerable precarious and dangerous situations, though he'd never hurt another person in a fight or while driving, nor had he been the victim of any crime. He and Richard were quiet drunks; they got their DUIs from being observed wavering across the yellow lines on county roads. As a result, both had spent weekends in jail.

According to local lore, when Kenny was still in high school, already a gifted mechanic, he worked at his dad's shop. His sisters weren't interested in the car repair business, and his brother, who always wanted to be a Marine, became one. Only Kenny inherited the magic gene for fixing cars, so he became the proud father's protégé. Kenny loved the way an engine could hum, the vibrating harmony of a perfectly calibrated transmission.

On the sixth day of the men's absence, an employee of Colorado's Department of Transportation was checking guardrails on that stretch of highway, 147 miles southwest of Denver, about 15 miles from our town. The woman thought she saw something shiny and metallic poking out of the scrub below, and called over a co-worker, who said it looked like the chassis of an old wreck. But the woman, who didn't remember seeing it on her last round six months before, decided to call the sheriff, just to check.

My multiple missing hours might have been spent unconscious at the bottom of a dip in the gravel road where I flew off the bike, going far too fast in the moonless dark. Or perhaps I roamed the woods, lost, wondering what to do. I will never know. Eventually, a man discovered me, threw my bicycle in the back of his pickup and drove a mile to the summer camp where I was working in the kitchen. Did I tell the pickup driver where I was staying? Or did he make an assumption, able to discern I wasn't a local. Did I speak, my accent giving me away? Maybe he took me there because it was the closest place that wasn't a private home, and, if a local, he would have known everyone in that isolated area. At the camp's office, they called for an ambulance; the nearest hospital was 60 miles away, and this was in an era before helicopters were used as often as they are now, here in rural Colorado, for a medical emergency.

After the sheriff got the fire department to send the "Jaws of Life" to the scene, and had plotted a roundabout but passable route to the wreck, the lawman, fire truck and EMT vehicle bumped along, scratching the hell out of the sheriff's front end, as he was in the lead. The woman from D.O.T. asked if she could accompany him ~ after all, it was her hunch that led to this multi-vehicle production, and she wanted to see what they found ~ but the sheriff refused. Because the county had no knowledge of a wreck in that location, it was

110

very likely they would find a body, he said ~ maybe a skeleton, depending on how long it had been there ~ and he wanted to spare her nightmares. The woman found his remarks condescending, but he was the law, so she didn't argue, vaguely relieved she would not have to witness a sight that might haunt her.

The car lay passenger side down, and when the sheriff, firemen and EMT team alighted from their vehicles, they thought surely no one could be alive inside that contorted metal carcass. The fireman said he would take the first look, as he would need to know if he would be able to use his equipment in the tight quarters beside the highway stanchion among the oaks. In his line of work, he'd seen skeletons, decomposed and decomposing cadavers, though usually he was called when bodies were still fresh, and, in the best circumstances, alive and salvageable.

He and one of the E.M.T. crew hacked through the scrub to get to the car, and they smelled Richard before they saw him. "Too late," said the fireman, who was thinking he shouldn't have come, because what if they needed a "Jaws of Life" to rescue a living person somewhere else, and his was the only one in the county, which was 100 miles square, more or less. The E.M.T. woman said, "Wait. There could be a passenger. Or passengers."

The fireman shrugged.

Then they heard something: a grunt or moan.

"What was that?" the woman asked.

"I'm on it," said the fireman, who flew into action, now grateful to be necessary and useful.

The sheriff, firemen and E.M.T. workers managed to get the driver's door open, as it was unimpeded, hindered only by gravity. The "Jaws" were necessary to get Richard's body out; he was a very large man, perhaps 300 pounds. After they managed that horrendous feat, the woman climbed into the car and found the living, though unconscious, Kenny, who had, by luck, been saved from smothering under the weight of his friend by an enormous rock piercing the roof of the car, wedging itself between the two men, creating an air pocket over the much smaller Kenny. His body temperature was 71° Fahrenheit.

Long after my accident, I was told that the Good Samaritan sat with me in his truck while waiting for the ambulance. My hunch is that I was conscious, probably in shock, but there is no particular reason for this supposition. What does it matter? Because it was summer, there was no danger of frostbite, and besides being dented and bruised, abrasions on my elbows and knees, my chief injury was to my mouth; evidently, I had fallen flat on my face, breaking some teeth and loosening others.

During his six extratemporal days, Kenny must have experienced withdrawal from alcohol. The shock, lowered body temperature and pain from various injuries might have minimized his transition to sobriety. These days, he is learning to walk with prostheses. Whenever possible, his siblings and father help with physical therapy. From time to time, Kenny still asks about Richard, and when he is reminded, gently, that Richard died in the accident, Kenny says, "That's right. I forgot."

In the nursing home where he is convalescing, Kenny has been visited by his ex-wife and two of his three children. Sometimes he forgets who they are, and, upon remembering, flashes a brilliant smile ~ or as brilliant as is possible with a damaged jaw ~ and declares how happy he is to see them.

Each decade since the bike accident, I have returned to teeth specialists ~ oral surgeons, prosthodontists, periodontists ~ to shore up my mouth. Every prosthesis has needed replacement. Now, I am trying implants, in the hope they will last me the rest of my days, thus putting an end to revisiting my own wreck every ten years, my tongue exploring the broken spaces and empty places where real teeth once lived.

Kenny may or may not acquire a new life in his post-accident, amputee world. At the garage one day, waiting for my car, I overheard Kenny's dad talking to another customer about his son's ordeal. "You know, after he started drinking so much in high school, I wouldn't let him work here anymore. It wasn't safe. I think he always resented that, but it was the right thing to do. Now, twenty-five years later, he's finally stopped." He snorted. "It only took the loss of his legs," he said, smiling a crooked smile.

A much older white-haired woman, the customer clenched his hand. "God is in this, you know," she said. "Another person might drink even more in your son's circumstances. But Kenny has seen the light."

"Maybe. We won't know, will we, until it all plays out. But I do remember him saying once, not long after he came out of the coma, something like, 'Richard gave his life for me.' "

"You see?" The woman nodded. "Richard died in order that your son might live. Kenny's new life was born out of that pain, like the rest of us, who owe our lives to Christ."

Sitting on a plastic chair, hiding behind the newspaper, I shook my head. Richard died because he was driving drunk and flipped the car off a cliff. That truth was clear enough. But why did Kenny live?

On the day of my accident, I had wanted to die. Untreated suicidal depression had eroded my will to persevere, and each day was an excruciating countdown: three hours, if I can just last three more hours, then I can go to sleep, and I'll wake up tomorrow, which will be better. But the tomorrows never improved, and the countdowns resumed in the mornings, my waking hours spent imagining various ways I might do myself in, how to disguise my death as an accident for my parents' sake. Their lives had not been easy, and for their youngest child to die a suicide would seem a brutal blow inflicted by me purposefully, which was not my intention. Rather, I just wanted to be put out of what felt like untenable misery.

Did Richard and Kenny want to die? Subconsciously, or drunkenly, or both, did Richard fly off the cliff in the car, believing they were levitating somehow, like the magic Rambler in the Harry Potter movies?

Which is the greater miracle: Kenny surviving or the Oldsmobile's flight over the guardrail instead of through it?

In my own case, the afternoon of the accident, I chose alcohol to ease the pain and succeeded marvelously. After months of darkness, I felt happy, thrilled, exuberant, able at last to leave myself behind. And the fall from the bike, the days in the hospital, the loss of teeth ~ all of it sprang from the blissful idea of flight. That night, on the road in the blackness, I believed I could fly on that bike, go so fast down the hill I would escape the pull of gravity, and travel out of time.

"HOW CAME THESE THINGS TO PASS?"

2013

Titania, Queen of the Fairies, in *A Midsummer Night's Dream*

My new obsession: reading the gun violence tally in the *New York Times* every day. On weekends, the writers suspend the daily report, only to amass a three-day toll for Mondays. In late March of 2013, the compilers of the data released the following message:

> "The volume of gun violence on the weekend can be overwhelming. To better acknowledge that sad truth, we have decided to change the nature of the Gun Report on weekends. Rather than highlighting only a handful of shootings, as we do during the week, we are going to try to give a more complete roundup of weekend gun violence. Our own synopsis of each shooting will necessarily be brief, but we will link to the original media source in case readers want more detail. Here is the first volume of our revised Weekend Gun Report."
>
> ~ Joe Nocera and Jennifer Mascia

Ever since learning of the existence of the Gun Report, I find myself drawn, horrified, to the brief descriptions, tersely stated, of shootings and killings all over these United States.

There are some days when it is more difficult to read about gun violence than others. Yesterday was awful, filled with senseless shooting and the deaths of children, some shot by accident, others on purpose.

"By accident" and "on purpose" are terms we use off-handedly, as if it were easy to tell the difference, but I find the more I read, the distinction is not always clear. An incident here in the rural town in which I've lived the last ten years makes that label especially difficult to discern.

"A 9-year-old girl was accidentally shot in the head and killed by someone inside her home while she was playing in her backyard in Oregon City, Ore., Sunday evening."

Like many others, including the *New York Times* reporters, I am particularly drawn to the deaths of children, especially in the wake of the Newtown shootings. Are children's deaths somehow more meaningful than the demise of adults? I think not. Yet ....

I read in the website linked to the Oregon death above that the "live-in boyfriend" was cleaning his handgun inside the home, and it remains to be seen whether charges will be filed. In the comments that follow, one reader urges lenience: accidents happen, she writes. Of course the "parents" do not necessarily include the shooter; did she not read the piece carefully, or did she choose to assume the live-in boyfriend was the father? Both will suffer from guilt for the rest of their lives, she offers, which is penalty enough. A response proclaims it is not an accident but negligence, a crime, like backing over a child in your driveway after failing to look first.

Why am I drawn to read the daily deaths by gun in the United States? My own life has not been shaped by guns but rather by their absence. In middle age, I moved to rural Colorado, where the proverbial gun rack in the pick-up is legion. I pass the shooting range every day on my way to school to drop my son. After Newtown, the sheriff and his "posse" ~ yes, these deputized men (no women), many of them retired law officers, volunteer to be in what is unironically called a posse ~ roam the halls of the small school, gun in holster. Do I feel safer when I teach my weekly AP English class, now that an armed and uniformed would-be protector is present, visible to all? Not especially. There was a policeman at Columbine, oft forgotten in the raucous, hostile discussion of what to do about school shootings. He did not stop the two boys from killing anyone. Nor is there any guarantee that one person with a gun in a building could in fact prevent another from firing his weapon. When Columbine occurred, I lived in Oregon; my pregnancy had been ecstatic, long-hoped-for, until April 20, 1999: when two boys shot a dozen classmates and teacher, then committed suicide at the high school which my grad school friend's children would soon attend, everything changed.

"A 13-year-old old girl was found dead inside a Jacksonville home
Saturday afternoon after a gun discharged while children ages
11, 10, 9 and 1 were playing with it."

Did the 1-year-old shoot the teenager? Are triggers difficult to pull for youngsters, so that they had to work really hard at their task? Was the oldest girl the babysitter, supposed to keep younger children safe while grown-ups were gone? The big sister?

"Several children ~ ages 13, 11, 10, 9 and 1 ~ were in the home
without adult supervision when a shooting occurred."

Titania Mitchell, a student at La Villa School of the Arts, Jacksonville, FL, is now deceased. Titania, named after the fairy queen in Shakespeare's "A Midsummer Night's Dream," a sparkling, gorgeous girl as seen in a photograph in the linked news story, will never again play her part.

Police have not said how the children got hold of the gun or who owns the home.

I live in the land of gun owners ~ not gun nuts, a term I recognize ~ but hunters and ranchers and even an old artist friend who used an ancient handgun to put a doe out of its misery after hitting her by accident with his car. She couldn't get up, so he drove home for the gun, then turned around to cover the 20 miles of dirt road to end her pain before the coyotes or mountain lions got her first.

Some people know how to use guns: to store them, to keep them away from children, like most families where I live. But even responsible adults find themselves confronting the kind of brutal violence that splatters itself across the daily gun report.

"A 2-year-old boy is recovering from a gunshot wound after
accidentally shooting himself in Gurley, Ala., Tuesday night.
Deputies responded to a home on Church Street around 7:20 p.m.
and found a child with a gunshot wound to the hand.
"Deputies said the unsupervised child shot himself. Deputies
notified the Department of Human Resources. No charges are
expected to be filed."

Unlike the story of Titania, the 9-year-old in my rural Colorado hamlet was accomplished with guns, a seasoned hunter who had taken multiple gun safety classes, as did all the children in his large, extended family. The five kids and their parents, cousins, grandparents, aunts and uncles knew their way around guns. Homeschooled, he and his next oldest sister were target shooting on a sunny day in March, an activity they did weekly when weather permitted. He was a good shot, with his child-size rifle, a gift passed down from father to each child. As the siblings grew, each abandoned the child-sized gun for a regular one. The youngest boy was quite small for his age, his arms not yet long enough for a standard rifle.

Their home, built by hand and perched at the edge of town, sits on a plot by itself at the end of a dirt road, which I walk daily with my dogs. Every morning I note how the isolation of the house might somehow have been a factor in Jimmy's death. Had they lived within town limits, as we do, with neighbors and regulations, they would not have been able to have targets in their backyard. But most folks here live out of town, where they can do as they please. This family had the best of both worlds: the convenience of town life without the shackling of town laws.

"Rekia Kid, 22, was shot in the stomach by her 2-year-old son at her
Lavinia, Tenn, home, Sunday. Investigators said the mother was
sleeping with her 3-week-old baby and toddler when the toddler
found a Glock 9-mm stored underneath Kid's pillow."

The family who lives on the outskirts of my town would never have a Glock or any kind of gun under a pillow. They would not let toddlers play with rifles. But Jimmy was 9 and not playing. Like every other week that March, and the March prior, he and his sister Evelyn (names are changed to protect the family's privacy) were practicing their accuracy on paper targets affixed to hay bales behind the house; they have 70 acres, and the nearest ranch is a mile south, so there's no danger of stray bullets hitting anyone. Because it is primarily treeless, they would have been able to see a cow or any creature nearing the target area.

> "A 6-year-old boy was accidentally shot in the head by his 4-year-old
> neighbor and killed in Toms River, N.J., Monday night. Brandon
> Holt and his young neighbor were playing in the younger boy's
> backyard when the preschooler went into his house, brought out a
> loaded .22- caliber rifle and shot the older boy in the head."

Relatives described the boys as playing "pretend shooting" before the actual shooting. Police removed several other weapons from the younger boy's home and are investigating whether the adults in the house were legally permitted to own the rifle.

Jimmy did not "pretend shoot." Nor did anyone here in his very large circle of family and friends. And yet, when he went to the basement to get more bullets, leaving his sister in the yard, where she shot an excellent bull's eye, he somehow managed to shoot himself.

> "A 3-year-old child in Sumter, S.C., is dead from an apparent self-
> inflicted gunshot wound. The shooting at the Magnolia Manor
> Apartments was reported around 10 a.m. Tuesday. Neighbors told
> police that the child shot the gun after finding it in the apartment.
> The boy was visiting from Georgia, and the Sumter County coroner
> is trying to contact the child's mother. No charges have been filed."

Yes, Jimmy was alone with his rifle, as he had been before, many times, and re-loaded on more occasions than anyone could count. He knew how the rifle worked; he and his dad had spent an entire evening examining every inch of it when he was 7 and given the gun, the youngest child and therefore the last to receive the bequest. His father gave the lecture he had given to every one of his children and had himself received long ago about how the rifle was not a toy, not to be played with, ever; to be kept unloaded at all times except for the family's annual deer hunts (and, if they were lucky, they might get a license for elk every few years); and for target practice. Period.

> "A 4-year-old girl was shot dead with a handgun inside a car outside
> her grandparents' home in Northwest Miami-Dade, Fla., Saturday
> night; a 6-year-old was found holding the weapon."

Jimmy obeyed his father's rules: he always walked with his rifle unloaded. He never played with his firearm as if it were a toy, though he'd had plenty of toy guns like so many boys, and girls, too, in this part of the country. It was target practice day, and he'd forgotten to bring the box of bullets outside. Usually, he reloaded the gun under his sister's supervision. But he'd left the box of bullets in the basement, in the gun safe, and had gone to retrieve it. Evelyn assumed he would bring the bullets back and reload as he always did, with her guidance. She hadn't noticed him taking the rifle into the house.

> "7-year-old Gavin Brummett died from a gunshot wound to the
> head in Saline County, Kan. after shooting a semi-automatic 9 mm
> handgun with his father and brother Friday evening."

Jimmy died from one shot. In the immediate aftermath of the death, no one wanted to talk about any of the gruesome details. I was at school, watching my son's 5th grade class demonstrate their volcanoes, made with plastic soda bottles, Mento mints and various special effects. We were in a field behind the school when we started hearing sirens speeding down Main Street. Because the school was in the way, we couldn't see whether they were fire engines or ambulances or sheriff's cars or all three. Everyone went back to watching the demonstrations, which lasted less than a minute each, the sometimes blood-colored liquid spewing out the sides of the constructed volcano, covering every object placed cleverly in its path. My son had asked for Monopoly hotels, those red plastic buildings, large compared to the little green houses, which he used as well. When the fake lava subsumed the structures, everyone applauded, including his classmate, Jimmy's first cousin, one of many relatives at the small school.

Surprisingly, the public address system came on: "Will all members of the Smith family please report to the office right away?"

His classmate, a girl who hadn't yet demonstrated her volcano, took off running. It couldn't be good news, if one believed the uneasy tone of the usually unflappable secretary over the loudspeakers. Not long afterward, we heard a helicopter, the Flight for Life orange mechanical bird heading toward the helipad. Could the call to all Smith family members be related to these emergency vehicles?

All the volcano demonstrators after the announcement looked scared, unable to summon up the pride in creation evidenced earlier in the hour. A group of parents buzzed with alarm. What could be happening? Children and adults held their collective breath.

"A man was charged with child endangerment in Cincinnati, Ohio.
Friday after his 3-year-old son pulled a loaded pistol out from underneath the man's mattress and shot himself in the arm."

Is it "child endangerment" to let a 9-year-old boy have his own child-sized rifle? Not around here. Later, everyone talked about what a horrible accident it was, a terrible loss; the general feeling in town reflected a deep sorrow. Jimmy was an impish kid, a soccer player and basketball nut. Sometimes he would "play up" on my son's soccer team, fearless about scooting between opposing team members' legs; he was so tiny he got away with it every time. Spectators would shake their heads but simultaneously admire his bravado: "That Jimmy!"

"A Twinsburg Township, Ohio, 16-year-old is hospitalized after he accidentally shot himself in the chest while cleaning a gun Saturday night."

If only Jimmy had shot himself in the chest, or some other body part than the head. Those of us unfamiliar with guns, with rifles, with loading and bullets, we had no idea how such an event could happen. Unlike the others in their grief, I was angry. How could this happen? Where were the parents? Why was he alone with a rifle and bullets? Those who've lived here longer simply nodded and said, "These things happen." At the funeral, Jimmy's mother said Jesus had called her youngest son to him, to sit at his feet in heaven. She seemed consoled by this thought, and I was reminded of the death of my nephew, two years old, dead from an incurable genetic Jewish disease, when his other grandmother had said, with total certainty, "God wanted him." For the rest of her life, she used her formidable will, secular and religious, to start and then sustain a foundation to fund research on this rare disease, so that others might not experience the same horror. Would Jimmy's mother or grandmother see a larger picture in Jimmy's death? I doubted it.

By the time of the funeral, held in the high school gym because it was the only place in town large enough to accommodate a thousand people, the parents seemed in shock, living in the new status quo but not believing it to be true: their five-child family was now a four-child one. The baby ~ the spoiled, sassiest, most beloved ~ was gone.

"A dad accidentally shot his son dead as he cleaned his gun in the family's living room. Christopher Stanlane, 34, was wiping down the loaded weapon at his home in Fairmont, N.C., Sunday when it discharged. The bullet hit his 10-year-old son, Christopher Stanlane Jr., who was watching television, in the back of the head. His 8-year-old daughter was also in the room. The boy was pronounced dead at the scene. No charges have so far been filed in the case."

Nearly a half-year after the killings at the Connecticut elementary school, everyone knows more about gun deaths than they did before: more guns are used for suicide than homicide. The annual death toll from guns has surpassed that of traffic fatalities, and so on. Was I the only person who thought he might have done it on purpose? Not that he intentionally committed suicide, but that he believed he could shoot a gun at himself and survive? He was only 9; maybe he didn't "get" the permanence of death. Maybe he didn't think he'd loaded the gun yet. He might have forgotten, been distracted by the arrangements of tools strung across the pegboard in constellations of neatness.

"A toddler accidentally shot himself in the chest and died while
  visiting relatives in Prichard, Ala., Sunday evening. An investigation
  is ongoing."

Jimmy didn't "accidentally shoot himself" was the thought I could not remove from my brain. How do you accidentally shoot yourself with a rifle? It seems very difficult to me, far more so than with a handgun, but I am a neophyte regarding firearms, so my understanding is primitive, if not inaccurate. I think of Hemingway shooting himself in the head with a rifle at 62 years old, a sufferer from depression all his life, suicide a family legacy, now continuing into his grandchildren's generation. It takes work to kill oneself that way. How did Jimmy manage it as a re-loading accident?

"A 3-year-old toddler accidentally shot himself in the head with a
  relative's gun, but was listed in stable condition at a Nashville, Tenn.
  hospital. The child, who has not been identified, was at home with his
  mother and his aunt when his aunt pulled out a gun. The toddler got a hold
  of the weapon and shot himself."

Not every gun report in the *New York Times* includes the kind of firearm used. The above 3-year-old probably was not handling a rifle, child-sized or otherwise. Far more deaths are attributable to handguns than rifles, as the NRA often reminds us. Handguns can look fake, like toys; pink pistols for women have been designed to be pretty, to fit in dainty handbags. It seems easier, somehow, to mistake a handgun for a non-lethal weapon because of its very portability, its snug fit in one's palm.

I shot a gun once, back in another lifetime, when I lived in Northern California with my boyfriend, whose friends had been to prison, some of whom dealt drugs, others engaging in various illegal activities. All those people had guns, though David, a vegetarian hippie, did not. One summer night we were visiting his new boss, the guy who organized a group of odd men and the occasional woman in painting government-subsidized apartments. He always paid in cash, and I didn't trust him or his soft-spoken wife, who had not been to prison, as far as I knew, but worshipped her tattooed and gangsterish husband. After dinner, we went into the backyard of the rural house, sipping our beers. Wanna shoot? his boss asked.

He set up cans on a makeshift bench at the edge of his property. There were houses nearby ~ not close ~ but it wasn't empty ranchland either. I didn't want to, but David, who was never good at saying no, said okay. He couldn't hit one can. Then the boss took the gun and fired, one shot after another decimating the row of cans. After setting it up again, he handed the gun to me. Oh, no thanks, I said, sure I didn't want to do it, annoyed that my boyfriend had done so when he was a peaceful man, a Nature worshipper who never hurt animals, even insects.

"Women are often better at it than men," said the boss, as if that fact would convince me. "Jolene is a way more accurate shot than I am. Here." He thrust the butt of the gun into my hand.

Why did I shoot? Because I never had before? Because I was vaguely drunk and therefore less inhibited? Because I somehow knew he wouldn't take no for an answer, which was surely why David had done it, perhaps shooting badly on purpose; I never knew.

I fired the gun and nearly passed out from the fear, the noise, the recoil. I had no idea it was such a physical experience. The men and the boss's wife laughed at my shocked expression. I hadn't shot anywhere near the cans, but no one seemed to mind.

"Go on. Try it again," Jolene urged, but I said no. I never wanted to have that feeling again: terror, reverberation from gunshot, that sense of power I held in my hand, knowing such a small object allowed me to kill: a person, an animal, anyone, anything ~ multitudes of living creatures.

The wife took the gun, and, like her husband, nailed each and every can. She seemed impervious to the intensity of the re-coil. It was as if she were still cooking dinner, or clearing the table ~ an everyday activity for her, unworthy of comment. As soon as we got in the truck to go home, I said I never wanted to go their house again; I was angry at myself for doing something I did not want to do.

Yeah, it made me uncomfortable too, David said, and that was that.

When that relationship ended, so did my involvement with people for whom guns were ordinary appendages.

Until now, raising my son in Colorado's semi-wilderness, a choice I made quite deliberately, leaving the city, where gangs roamed, and armed robbers regularly stole cars, invaded homes, broke into pharmacies for prescription drugs to feed their habits.

Here, where the deer roam nightly across the track and football fields, peppering the grass with their droppings, my son was experiencing the death of his soccer-teammate by firearm. An accident.

"A baby sitting on the floor of an apartment building in Richmond, Calif., was seriously injured Thursday during a shooting that took place 30 yards away. A 1-year-old boy was taken to the hospital with a neck wound after an as-yet-unidentified gunman fired at a man in the street."

I wonder how a boy who supposedly knew his way around a rifle, a kid-sized rifle at that, managed to blow his head off. Might it have been some sort of stupid prank, as if he thought it would be funny, somehow, similar to other pranks he had pulled in the past, just taken one step farther?

Today's report, another weekend gone, informs us:

"Cody R. Hall, 4, died from a single gunshot wound in an accidental shooting in Donald, Ore.

"A 2-year-old child reached into his father's pocket, grabbed a gun and shot himself at his grandparents' home in Greenville County, S.C.

"10-year-old Eri Raya is clinging to life after being shot multiple times at a family member's birthday party in North Highlands, Calif."

FOUR PROTAGONISTS, ONE AUTHOR
2007

Upon reading the latest version of my Jonestown novel, a new friend remarks, "It seems you're closest to Marceline of the four main characters."

"What?!" I sputter. "How can you say that? She's the one I have the most trouble with!"

Autumn. The fourth year of my life-in-Jonestown commences, the novel wending its way through a final round of publishers courtesy of my valiant agent, its fifth title ~ *Fathom These Events: Jonestown, a Novel*; *Fathoming Jonestown*; *Jonestown Perfume*; *Resurrection City*; *Paradise Undone* ~ and umpteenth draft.

However, the four main characters have remained the same throughout. Two come from Jonestown history: Marceline Jones and the Guyanese ambassador to the United States, whom I call Virgil Nascimento. Two are of my own invention: Truth Miller, a white female Temple member who works in the radio room at the San Francisco Geary Boulevard headquarters on the last day of Jonestown; and Watts Freeman, a black Temple member who escapes on that final day and spends a great deal of time during the next 30 years trying to describe to the media what Jonestown was like.

When I started researching this book, I knew Marceline would be crucial to the story. Although there's a dearth of information about her in Jonestown literature, she was integral to Peoples Temple in its rise as well as its demise. But what had I in common with Marceline Baldwin Jones?

Nothing on the surface. She married and stayed with her man to the bitter-tasting end. In contrast, I have never married nor wanted to, though I gave birth to one fabulous son in 1999. For 29 years, she remained in the shadow of her charismatic life partner, despite the fact that without her massive energy, devotion and love, Peoples Temple might not have accomplished all the good it did, and what evolved or devolved might have done so in a different form ~ whether more or less toxic, we shall never know.

131

For me, a woman taking a husband's name has always been anathema ～ akin to the practice of slavery ～ and the actions I have undertaken thus far in my 47 years (Marceline was 51 when she died, Jim 47) have been my own, with the name I was born with, for better and worse. As a feminist, I found the protagonist Marceline my most painful act of character inhabitation.

On the other hand, Virgil, like me, devotes himself to the life of the mind and looks to literature and art for answers. Unlike me, he exists solely in this realm and lacks a grounding in the gritty business of daily life, such as caring for a child, for instance, or tending to family.

This deficiency proves integral to his doom. However, I could easily nestle in Virgil's brain: he wants answers to problems, like most of us, and without them, he despairs. The fact that he ends his life as a murderer did not keep me from empathy.

Truth (née Elizabeth) Miller is also an ideologue, though unschooled at the beginning of the story. She meets Jim Jones and joins the Temple in 1970, when she is 18. For decades, she huddles under his political umbrella ～ even after Jonestown. However, she is not exactly a brainwashed follower. Until joining Peoples Temple, she sees herself as an outsider, like me, someone who never fits in, someone who always has to make her own way. Like me, she is passionate and at times excessive. She is loyal ～ to a fault ～ and fiercely devoted to her son. Her little boy, Cuffy, has more than a few traits in common with my own child. Although she never entirely sheds her naiveté, Truth comes to value education and balance as she ages.

While Watts might seem the longest leap for me ～ he grows up in poverty amid the projects of Los Angeles, and comes from a fractured family life depleted by drugs, alcohol and racism ～ I like him most of the four and hope I share with him a love of the truth and an aversion to lies. More than the other three, he is practical, and guided ～ once free of narcotics ～ by common sense. Like most of us, he is not noble or valiant, but he embraces life in all its horror as well as its wonder. Like me, he is a storyteller and wants to communicate what he perceives to be the truth about Jonestown and the people who died there. He is especially concerned about those who remain, thirty years later in 2008 ～ when I hoped my book would be published ~ gravely misunderstood and/or forgotten by the American public.

So how is it that my new friend could think me most closely connected to Marceline? The wife and mother and stand-by-your-man-while-he-cheats, behind-your-man-while-he-gets-all-the-credit heroine?

When I think of what is best about Marceline ~ her great love for others, her loyalty to the elders and the sick and the children ~ then I wish to be someone with those same traits. When I consider her terrific energy and desire to help other human beings, I hope I have a fraction of her will. When I reflect on the way she took in so many children and old people who were not blood relations and treated them as her own beloved family, I aspire to such largesse of heart.

But when I imagine the last day of Jonestown, and her *apparent* ~ though not proven ~ lack of resistance to the poisoning plan, to the mass murders and suicides of nearly a thousand people, two thirds of them elderly or children ~ then I pray I haven't the slightest drop of Marceline Baldwin Jones residing anywhere inside me.

Intuitively, I relate to the surviving narrators of *Paradise Undone*, Truth and Watts, who, like Ishmael in *Moby Dick*, live to testify about an ordeal now part of American mythic history, and testify in order to live.

WELCOME, NOW LEAVE
2004

"Close the gate behind you" is the cattleman's rule around here.

It makes sense: keep your cows in and your neighbor's out. Coming and going, you learn how to gauge each minute as you stop the car, run for the gate, unhook the chain, drive through, stop again, run back and re-chain.

But what about one's desire to shut it tight forever? I am reminded of the signs once popular in the Northwest: "Welcome to Oregon. Now Go Home."

Here in Colorado's high country, some feel similarly. After a dozen years as an annual visitor, now a resident for the last three winters in Custer County, I bristle at the sight of new construction down the road. In the last three months, two homes have risen just in the rutted stretch of county road between the cabin and the highway. "For Sale with Sewer and Power Ready-To-Go" signs pepper a new subdivision south of town.

At a recent dinner, friends discussed the unwillingness of locals to pay taxes toward improving the roads. "Washboards keep the realtors out," said one old-timer, who understands the impulse. As do I.

On our five-and-a-half-mile trek from cabin to schoolbus stop on Route 69 South, my son asks why our road isn't paved, why we bump along so vigorously, the sound of wheels skimming rocks dinning out his mystery on tape.

"Honey, if they paved all the way up here," I yell, "can you imagine how many neighbors we'd have?"

Our 35-acre plot comprises a tiny fraction of a ranch subdivided decades back, one of the first in the county to go. As local wisdom has it, ranchers make more money from Houston speculators than Texas longhorns. Trophy houses about the ridges, builders parking 5,000-square-foot eyesores face-first into the wind, scoring the buyer's million-dollar view of the Sangres while bruising everyone else's with a high-ceilinged white elephant, which sits empty 50 weeks out of every year.

While candidates for county commissioners stake out their positions on growth, it's hard to locate the golden mean. Instinctively, we want to slam the gate behind us on the way in, keeping the classes small, the bikes unlocked in front of the library and supermarket where everyone knows our children by name.

For those whose families homesteaded South Colony in the 19th century, I belong to that obnoxious collection of newcomers provoking this ranching community with big city ideas, though I have gladly left most urban ways behind me.

Yet I am sympathetic to their position, nostalgic for what this world once looked like.

At the same time, new blood infused into the life of our town makes for an expanded public library and fresh donations of DVDs, books on tape and diverse children's literature. The local theater plays foreign and independent films one night a week. At the café, one can sip an excellent cup of coffee while listening to public radio and checking e-mail on the Wi-Fi. None of this was true a dozen years ago, when first I spent a summer here, nor two decades back when I originally stepped foot in this valley, openmouthed with awe.

"It's so quiet," visitors say, listening intently to the silence. The wind sidles around the cabin before dashing down into the arroyo. Antelope and mule deer camouflage themselves against the grassy slopes. At night, constellations gleam inside the dark bowl of sky. Coyotes yip beneath the hills.

Last year, someone new was at last able to afford her retirement dream and move in down the furrowed one-lane "avenue," which suddenly I must share with another. Now vehicles not my own sometimes cruise the hill, as often as once a day. Our dogs have a new truck to herd. We adjust. The gate remains open.

A WRITER'S JOURNAL, PART II
2007

Whatever we inherit from the fortunate
We have taken from the defeated
What they had to leave us ~ a symbol:
A symbol perfected in death.
T.S. Eliot's "Little Gidding," fourth of *Four Quartets*

Ten years ago, wandering the fields of this same valley, but then *in* the Sangres, rather than looking at them from the other side, as I do now ~ a crucial distinction ~ I read, listened to, memorized, and studied Eliot's *Four Quartets*, seeking within the long poem a kind of answer. That fall, overseas, I had suffered a crisis of meaning, and the way out of crisis ~ either suicide or its alternative, to go on living ~ needed explication. For a solid month, I contemplated the former with certainty, but despite a kind of clarity that recommended death, I opted for the latter.

Once again home in the mountains, I began to read, unable to create anything new, able only to record the words of others in my notebook, needing to find meaning in literature, in something, anything. At 36, I realized I had to part with the atheism that had directed me thus far because it served no longer. Eliot's poem became my prayer, not because it gave me hope ~ though parts of it did ~ but because it described the complexity of my particular hopelessness, and proposed a resolution: not a solution, not an exit, but a restoration of the entire picture, of which I was seeing only part. The above stanza continues:

And all shall be well and
All manner of thing shall be well
By the purification of the motive
In the ground of our beseeching.

What does it mean? And how, you are probably wondering, can I possibly find beauty in a poem written by a misogynist, racist, anti-Semitic imperialist (pig)? I asked myself these questions too. And yet. *Four Quartets*, Eliot's last poem, talks back to the early poems: some of them hate-filled, some cruel, many ~ especially *The Wasteland* (obvious by its title) ~ full of despair. Can a human re-invent himself or herself? Is redemption possible?

Yes.

I am closer to seeing the entire picture of Jonestown, not just its most despairing facets ~ though I see those too ~ while the personal issues of the self ~ myself ~ have been subsumed by the grander issues of the world.

When people ask why I am writing about Jonestown, I am tempted to respond that a better question would be, "Why *not* Jonestown?" Every subject worth writing about, worthy of strenuous effort to understand, finds a home in Jonestown. Love, for instance. Justice. History. Equality. Kindness. Humanity. Violence. Cruelty. Despair. Death. All the "isms" are there: racism, sexism, capitalism, Socialism, post-colonialism, among others. Power hunger. Resistance to power. Solidarity and cliquishness. Greed and selflessness. Altruism and selfishness. Murder and heroism. The love of parents for children and the killing of children by parents. The healing of the sick and a homicidal "elixir," mixed by a doctor and dispensed by nurses.

Last year I wrote about my reading list, playing with the names of titles that showcased Jonestown in all possible variations. As the third autumn begins, I find my reading list contains fewer and fewer titles featuring "Jones."

Darkness at Noon; Destroying the World to Save it: Aum Shinrikyo, Apocalyptic Violence, and the New Global Terrorism; Existentialism from Dostoyevsky to Sartre; The Collected Wisdom of Heraclitus; The Gift; Gilead; The Bonds of Love: Psychoanalysis, Feminism and the Problem of Domination; Strategies for Survival: The Psychology of Cultural Resilience in Ethnic Minorities; Cities on a Hill; American Utopias; This Far By Faith: Stories from the African American Religious Experience; Guyanese Boy; The Kaywana Trilogy; Brave New World; We; The Possessed.

And, over and over, as I climb up and down these hills, *The Myth of Sisyphus*. When others ask how I can stand to re-live such a horrendous moment in American history, I say that I can stand it because I am here, in this valley, where I was spared, in the "ground of my beseeching." The morning after that storm a decade ago, the road was littered with telephone poles, whole groves had toppled, cars and homes caved in by the wind's fury; I was alive. At last I understood there was something more powerful than human will and was glad of it.

Arthur Koestler's hero Nicholas Rubashov of *Darkness at Noon*, a Cold War classic, says that suicide is a kind of inverted vanity. While I respect those who died in Guyana on November 18, 1978, I find Koestler's notion applicable to the Jonestown dead. Rubashov's opposite number, in the next cell, declares, "Honor is to live and die for one's belief." But Rubashov, who will shortly be executed for "counterrevolutionary acts" by the state he helped to create replies, "Honor is to be useful without vanity."

Are my motives "pure" as in Eliot's phrase? I don't know what purity means. Every day, I read and write, harvesting moments of clarity regarding those who left us in the Guyanese jungle in Jonestown, the ground of their beseeching.

SACRED AND PROFANE DANCES
1976

He called us "the three primas," and we loved our title, dancing furiously in the converted garage/studio, old mono record player on the floor humming its Debussy beneath the sound of rain drumming an antithetical beat on the tin roof. As we pirouetted, sweat hit the mirror, and we fouettéd again and again, our taskmasters driving us relentlessly until, sore and stiff, we hobbled the 50 feet to the dining hall for lunch and, later, dinner. It rained all summer, except the day of our outdoor performance, a miracle at the time and in retrospect still, as if the gods ~ definitely Dionysian ~ were rooting for our triumph.

Cristóbal named us and we thrived, working hard to please him, but Carol frowned whenever she heard him say it. "Primas!" she'd snap in disgust. "As if we needed one more prima in the world, much less three." Once, she'd been one herself, with the telltale upright carriage and rigid posture of the classically trained ballerina. None of us would turn professional ~ none of us was great ~ but we trained six days a week as if we were, Carol and Cristóbal our bad and good cops, respectively, both shrieking "Cheeks! Cheeks! Cheeks!" at the top of their lungs, urging us to tighten our gluteus maximus muscles as we leapt and spun and jetéd all around the shining wooden floor, pretending we were covering real distance on the wide lawns overlooking the lake, the intended stage for our performance on Parents' Day.

We were 17, 16 and 13, all of us from pricey East Coast suburbs of one sort or another. Amelia, the eldest, me in the middle, and Maria the baby, definitely the most talented and least serious among us. In private, we called ourselves "the three cheeks." On the bus up from Manhattan, Maria and I discovered we lived in the same Long Island suburb, though we had not known one another before camp. It was my third summer at Long Lake Creative Arts and Work Camp, Maria's and Amelia's first and last.

Later, I was told Cristóbal and Carol had married one another at 18, both escaping repressive families elsewhere ~ his in Columbia and hers in Kansas ~ for the dancer's life in New York City. They stayed married all their lives, though both had partners of the same sex and did not resemble any married couple I'd ever observed within the affluent boundaries of West Egg, the name F. Scott Fitzgerald came up with for Great Neck, New York. What did we know about sexuality, other than that everyone had some? Until that summer I'd been ugly and invisible, but suddenly at 16, it was as if I'd been born anew in the country of desire. Male counselors flocked to me to flirt, all of them several years my senior. I barely understood how the process worked, except that the borrowed yellow leotard on my braless body attracted attention every time I wore it, when my black ones grew unwearably stinky, and laundry day was still to come. Attired in leotards and sweatpants from breakfast through dinner, I wore no makeup, no perfume. After meals, I fed the horses and mucked out the stables, which, that wet summer, were ankle deep in mud.

Amelia and I shared the "counselors-in-training" room in the Main House, once the centerpiece of a grand estate. Because I was a Long Lake veteran, I knew how one could enter or escape the room by means of the low, flat roof and mostly sturdy trellis, evading the ears of counselors in the adjacent hallway. One midnight in late July, as Amelia and I lay on our narrow cots discussing our difficulties with Cristóbal's choreography, combined with the lack of practice in our actual performance space, the window slid up. A sheet of light rain briefly sprayed Amelia, whose bed abutted the wall overlooking the roof, before a male body appeared, silhouetted in the frame. Artie the clarinet counselor, who had so admired my yellow leotard just that afternoon, was followed by Josh, who taught painting.

"Shhhhhhh!" Artie placed a forefinger on Amelia's lips as she rose in alarm, ready to scream. "We've come to give you massages."

Since he'd climbed into the room onto Amelia's bed, he stayed there, while Josh, after slipping on the wet slate tiles, managed to hoist himself in and cross the narrow aisle to mine. Unexpected yet entirely natural, somehow, this nocturnal visitation, in which some previously unrealized instinct informed me that Artie was in the wrong bed, so I said his name and stretched my arm toward him. As if in a pre-arranged *pas de deux*, he accepted my hand, sliding his smooth fingertips up my forearm, and followed it back to me, while Josh exchanged my bed for Amelia's.

144

Had the married counselor couple down the hall heard the sounds of our strenuous massage session, what would they have done? Inquired about birth control, perhaps. Since arriving, I'd been in love with the man of the couple, who had a curiously female name ~ Lynn ~ and a delicate grace to all his gestures, a quietness of speech. I liked his wife too, Jody, with her lean runner's body and no-nonsense candor.

No one in the Main House was very old: Lynn and Jody the elders at 25, if that, Artie and Josh both 21 that year and reveling in their freedoms. It was rumored, and later confirmed, that Artie spent the remainder of that summer not only with me but with Pierrot, the drama counselor, alternating nights. And Josh, as the proverb went, chased everything that moved. Rain prevailed, keeping the grass a rich green; outdoor amorousness was difficult while not impossible, and the summer purred with yearning from beginning to end.

During the first week of camp, sensibly accepting that Lynn adored his admirable Jody, I had turned my attention to Don, one of two maintenance men. So shy he could barely speak, his reserve drew me to him, long dark hair an enticement to my empty hands. We didn't have our first conversation until the day he quit, he and the other maintenance man having decided to spend the summer driving cross-country instead of fixing outdated plumbing seven days a week, deep in mildew most of the time. Amelia and I stole away to their quarters to say goodbye, the old boathouse a flight of stone steps below the rest of camp. When I heard Greg Allman's mournful voice singing "Melissa," I launched, myself, weeping, onto Don's lap.

The lack of future summoning our inexperienced selves to action, we kissed and hugged and held hands all the way to the parking lot. As their Karman Ghia bumped up the dirt road, I grieved the taste of his affection and its immediate loss.

Parents' Day dawned cloudless and warm. My family didn't make the seven-hour drive to visit, which I preferred, since I felt free without them, needing my annual escape to the North Country to breathe. Josh had designed our costumes as loose togas silk-screened with Matisse-like cutouts in bright oranges, yellows and greens against the white. We were barefoot, black leotards beneath, no tights or leggings to constrain us. Instead of the tinny sound of the phonograph in our studio, Debussy boomed out over the P.A. system, the same that woke us every morning with a cowbell, unfurling the French composer's creation over the hundred or more acres of Long Lake Camp. When the first chords began, harpist Nicanor Zabaleta fingering strings from the air, it seemed, the deep blue sky itself offered up the first movement, the *danse sacrée*.

We three primas jetéd out from behind a copse of maples in Cristóbal's original composition, our legs stretching wider and wider as if to encompass the lake, reaching and reaching. It all made sense now, the way he made us move, how we heard "Cheeks! Cheeks! Cheeks!" echoing inside us, our elders' wisdom absorbed at last. I fell, rolled and recovered. The audience clapped spontaneously as I rose to join the others in the *danse profane*, all three of us unable to do anything but smile and leap and enter Debussy's romance in the air.

That fall, Maria and I took the train to the city and found our way to Cristóbal's loft, which he shared with André, his sweetheart of many years, the son of Long Lake's director. Inside, potted trees grew two stories high, reaching to the skylight. A huge makeup table was crowned by multi-colored lights around the mirror, a life-sized female plastic doll's legs stretched above it in glorious extensions. Cristóbal brewed us jasmine tea in a pot from Nepal, wearing a holey T-shirt that exposed his lovely shoulders and taut, muscled torso. He was thrilled by our visit, but not our admitted failure to keep dancing. The way he hugged us goodbye made us long for soaring, for touch, for everything the summer had promised.

Eventually, Artie undertook the deflowering he'd come for that night in the Main House. During Christmas break from college, he ushered me into his bedroom in his parents' home in Queens and locked the door. Though I'd prepared with a just-acquired diaphragm, he used a condom too, and while his father played ragtime on the piano 25 feet away, I whispered an unceremonious goodbye to virginity, which I'd never valued in the first place. The event was far less memorable than the full-body massage I'd received back at camp, while Amelia experienced hers in the other bed, a thunderstorm serenading us for hours, the window remaining open.

Decades later, I learned that both Cristóbal and André died of AIDS, Cristóbal nursing his love for three years, then Carol moving in to nurse Cristóbal for another three. Six months after my evening at Artie's, his piano-playing father would hang himself in the basement with a dog leash, where Artie would discover him, searching for a carton of sheet music he never found. Artie never slept with men again, possessed by the notion that his brief bisexuality had somehow engendered his father's suicide.

At 50, I finally own the Debussy after years of trying to identify and locate the very orchestration we danced to in the sun reflecting off Long Lake. After Artie, there were many men, a few women, until I came to know myself as a happy loner and loving mother of one son. The harpist still summons romance from the air, only this air is Colorado dry, my open, treeless acreage soughing in high altitude wind.

The snow-topped Sangres dwarf us here, so unlike the Adirondacks' soft green mounds, gentling dancers and spectators alike in a respite from the rain.

THE BELOVED ESSAYS
2011
Part I

After I send him a photograph of my home, he emails back:

"Wait a minute! You live in this cabin?! No way you live in this out-of-some-movie cabin?! No way! Okay, can I be your friend?! Please? Please? Okay, I am overwhelmed with this! You should write something romantic out there."

In reality, my little cabin has nothing remotely cinematic about it. Compost toilet, perennial mice, flies, a water system that has broken down every winter for seven years and counting, so that many months of each year are devoted to "hauling water," a rural chore unfamiliar to me in my previous existence as a city-dwelling professor living on every grid that exists.

When some colleagues came to visit, they uniformly agreed, "I could *never* live out here." I knew they weren't talking about the compost toilet, because they hadn't yet entered the cabin.

But my beloved, also a writer, was thrilled when he stepped out of the car after "that long rocky road," as he often calls it. "I bet I could finally finish something I started out here," he said, imagining life off the grid not as a hassle, nor as an interminable drive over excessively wash-boarded roads away from what some call "civilization."

But another reality entirely.

A place where one can "hear oneself think."

Pronghorn antelope roam the meadows, sometimes seating themselves at the edges of the road, taking in the morning sun-warmed dirt. Every summer one male, cast off by his group, searches for a new herd. His horns sometimes appear over the crest of the hill a mile from the cabin. He is my sentinel, alerting me to the nearness of home. Surely it's not the same youngster each of these seven years, but I sense a similar melancholy in these boys. Cast out, seeking community. Perhaps some of my visitors feel the same when they come to this wide open space without trees. Perhaps they feel exiled from someplace rather than welcome in this vast landscape.

Never in my life had I imagined living without trees! I moved here from the excessively verdant Pacific Northwest, where moisture drips incessantly, moss burgeons across rooftops and sidewalks, and the forest overwhelms the trees.

No obvious shelter here, no deterrent to the relentless wind that sweeps the acreage, picking up lightweight rocking chairs from the deck and smashing them, piecemeal, onto the scrub. And yet, there's something elemental about that openness to sky and cloud and weather of every kind. The hawks glide the thermals and sometimes land for a kill: mice or voles or moles or prairie dogs. Out here, you have to make peace with the critters, or you'll never survive a year.

Inside, the walls are adorned with my son's drawings, Aboriginal prints from Pitjantjatjara, bark cloth from Fiji, and hundreds of Crayola-bright bundles of yarn for rugmaking, which also help to pad the uninsulated half-log cabin. Yet a gale can blow through the cracks and hurl parti-colored wool onto the floor, lifting the curtains from the glass.

What will we look forward to out those single-paned windows? Spectacular cloudscapes, storms that linger in summer, casting hail on the nasturtium flourishing in pots lining the deck. This year, mice gobbled my germinating buds ~ right on the kitchen counter!

New problems announce themselves regularly, and one has to be innovative in creating solutions. Nature is in charge here, not people. I prefer it that way. He likes the coyotes infiltrating the night silence, and the way unexplained lights pierce the dark. Looking ahead to winter, our fantasies of being snowed in bode well for when the roads slick up, and drifts lace the ridges, when we human beings are really, truly, beyond control.

Part II

My beloved calls it the "thinking cabin," or sometimes, the "writing shack." I had meant to name it "Le Cabanon," after my professor's private study in the South of France. Behind his home in the hills, he directed me down a path through the lavender to a little outbuilding, maybe 15 x 20 square feet. Inside, I felt like I had entered a sacred space: very simple, sparse, holy. A desk and chair, some book shelves, a narrow cot on which to take a nap. One summer, I took that trip to visit my University of Denver creative writing teacher, William Wiser, perhaps 25 years ago. His wife was French, and while in Colorado, he lived in a tiny studio in South Denver, where he invited students to share a meal, a glass of wine. He was humble and quiet, a respected through not famous writer of literary fiction.

When he and Michelline picked me up in their "Deux Chevaux" at the train station in Cannes, I had no particular expectations of their home. Some place unassuming, I thought, unpretentious. Bill didn't drive, and Michelline sped through the hill town of Grasse and out into the country, tearing up the dirt, as there was no pavement, not unlike the roads to my mountain home outside of Westcliffe. But there was no Westcliffe in my life then; I was a graduate student in Denver, preparing for life as a professor of English, a writer of books, a dweller of cities.

He kept telling her to slow down as the tiny tin-like car-contraption made surprising speed, and the passageways were more like paths, only one car-width wide. Michelline made no allowance for the fact that some other crazy French driver might be ascending the hill toward us on the other side.

Nevertheless, we arrived with our lives intact, and there I ran out of superlatives. Their home was spacious without being large, their furnishings tasteful, quiet, tall windows overlooking the pastoral vista we managed to survive during our hair-raising trip from town. But it was "Le Cabanon" I coveted. His space, a writer's home away from home, though close enough to return for lunch, a cup of tea.

More truthfully, I coveted the life: a home in the country, not to mention the French countryside, a good job teaching reasonably intelligent graduate students during a short academic year ~ an Edenic life for a person who just wanted to write. Still in my twenties, I did not envision such a future for me, but I gladly took the offered model for my dreams.

In life, as in art, the end of the story doesn't usually match the intentions of its creator.

Dutifully, I taught my students in the city of Portland, and drove for days every summer to reach my haven in the Sangres ~ a rented adobe in the Huérfano one summer, a custom cabin in Bear Basin for another. I parked my manual typewriter on various surfaces: a splintery picnic table, a rickety dock overlooking a cow pond, a kitchen counter with a view of hungry chipmunks devouring birdfeed around a fire ring.

Time passed.

In 2004, on my second sabbatical, my then four-year-old son and I moved into our renovated one-room cabin in the Wet Mountain Valley, ostensibly for a year. Le Cabanon did not yet exist, not even as an idea. The year became two, as I labored on an historical novel I could not stop writing. The sabbatical became an unpaid leave, and then I quit my job, so we could stay in the mountains. I sold my home in Portland; real estate in a desired urban location being what it was, I made enough to invest in yearly plumbing upgrades on the cabin, slowly replacing a system one plumber kindly called "Mickey Mouse" at best. If the water keeps running through the winter of 2011, it will be a first!

The wooden model for sale at Greenleaf Forest Products in Westcliffe had a label reading "The Chapel" on its front door. It had a loft and several tall vertical windows that opened, in addition to two elevated round ones that didn't, and a charming front porch just big enough for a rocking chair.

My son didn't like my proposed froufrou French title for the Chapel, and when his cousin Benjamin came to visit just after it was delivered, my nephew the stand-up comedian proposed the perfect eponym: the Benny.

No matter what we call it, the thinking cabin offers a retreat from our retreat, a space for creation or merely escape, a meditation room, an extra bed with circular views looking east and west, another kind of Cabanon, scented by sage, attended by antelope.

Part III

Rats

Until this summer, I had never seen the mythical packrat, though I'd heard tales aplenty, down at the Anonymous Artists of America commune in Huérfano County. "Oh, you can't go in that cabin," a member told me, "the packrats have taken over." He pointed to an ancient hippie abode sagging off a cliff. I looked in the windows and saw only mounds of stuff: unidentifiable heaps of matter pillowed all the way to the sill.

Seven years in our cabin, and of the rodent family, only sweet little mice had visited. The first clue was lollipop wrappers. My son had been given a few Tootsie Pops, and he deposited them on a table for another day. In the morning, I found three crisp wrappers on the floor, but no candy. Odd. Then the scat appeared, at least five times bigger than mice poop. I began to worry. One night, while playing Scrabble on the bed, my son suddenly yelled, "What was that?"

Out my right eye, I, too, sensed movement. Since our solar was down ~ awaiting new batteries ~ I used a flashlight to peer behind the fridge, and just there, beside the pilot flame, was a creature, a hundred times larger than any mouse, staring me down.

What to do? My son wanted to pummel it with a golf club. I said no. Maybe I could knock it out with some sort of toxic spray ~ deodorant? ~ then transport its unconscious body to a new home in the distant trees. I sprayed. We waited.

After five minutes, we wrestled to budge the refrigerator: no body. That rat had fled! So I bought traps: live ones as well as the killing kind, and set both.

Clearly, we could not all cohabitate in our tiny cabin: my son, myself, the dogs, and the hugest rodent in the universe. A day later, one red woodrat met its end behind the stove, its bushy tail as long as its dead body, squirrel-like. Could there be more? I re-set the trap and found Junior the next day. So far, end of rat story.

Porcupine

You already know how this story ends: the porcupine wins. My Beloved and his two sons traveled from Denver for their first visit to our foreign country life. Dinner went fine, all the boys getting along. Afterward, they sang along to the pop music their father and I can't stand. We were pleased, believing our first attempted Brady Bunch night had gone well, when the door burst open, and all three boys screamed. Looking up from our books, we saw Fred, my rescue-dog-with-severe-anxiety-on-doggy-Prozac, careering around the room in pain, his face a bloody pincushion.

Shock.

Earlier, I'd heard the dogs barking and assumed they were chasing a rabbit. But here was Fred, a veritable monster, howling, attempting with his paws to get the quills out of his face, pushing them in deeper.

Immediately, I went into high calm emergency mode. After coaxing Fred to me, I linked his collar to a cable, hooking him to the porch railing with little room to move. We wrapped his body in a rug, trying to soothe him. My Beloved held him while I used the needle-nose pliers, hating the task but knowing I had to do it. Midnight before Labor Day, we were 90 miles from any emergency vet.

When Fanny showed up, she had maybe seven quills in her face, which I quickly extracted. (She's my smart girldog.) After three hours attempting to remove the porcupine's weapons ~ there had to be at least 200 of them, in Fred's mouth, cheeks, ears, muzzle ~ while he resisted, once slipping out of his collar to run away and return, I gave up. Perhaps I'd pulled 30 or 40, but dozens and dozens remained. Clearly, he would have to be sedated. The boys slept on the deck under the stars, exhausted Fred cabled where he couldn't rub against anything. My Beloved and I did not sleep.

At dawn, we left for Pueblo, where a wonderful emergency hospital fixed Fred to the tune of $600. His right cornea was abraded, but when the vet told me about another dog quilled right through the pupil and blinded, I felt fortunate.

Today, Fred is fine, his eye fully recovered. I am poorer, and the new blended family weathered its first emergency. The porky-pine, as the boys call him, roams free, indifferent to the dumbness of dogs, ever secure behind his natural armor.

CABIN-BOUND
2006

Getting here at dusk, the car serpentined into a drift up to its axles. As we were in sight of the cabin, I didn't worry. Yet. After two weeks in town, my seven-year-old son and I were eager to get back to our home ~ to return to open skies, no neighbors, antelope, uninterrupted mountain views, etc.

Laptop and DVDs, books and decks of cards in my shoulder bag, we set off toward the red roof capping our 780 square feet of drafty, cozy home. Although the shortest distance between two points is a straight line, that equation doesn't translate in drifts a few feet high, nor serious wind in dropping temperatures, and failing light. The dogs jumped from hillock to hillock with grace and ease, enjoying the adventure after being cooped up in a fenced yard for too long. Initially, I too enjoyed the adventure, until the sun sank behind the Sangres, the house as distant as ever, looking more like a blur than a building.

"This is how dumb city people die," I scold myself, remembering with trepidation the death earlier this winter of a San Francisco man, adrift in the snowy hills of Southern Oregon, seeking help for his car-bound family after getting stuck on an unfamiliar mountain road.

Like the dogs, my son isn't complaining, nor is he thinking about the inherent danger of our situation. Frostbite, for starters. Naturally, I left our good snowboots inside the cabin, and our flimsy footwear is completely inadequate to navigate deep drifts, some of them nearly the height of my child. I fear for his toes. In the worst-case scenario, we will freeze to death.

How many stories have I read about people dying in blizzards within spitting distance of their homes? Countless. My favorite, "Wickedness," by Ron Hansen, recounts the major Nebraska whiteout of 1888, in which a record number of people perished.

Staying cheerful as I tire ~ I am 39 years older than my son ~ I say things like, "Almost there!" and "Look, there's the birdfeeder!" while thinking what a lousy mother I am. At least our coats are warm, our hands dry in gloves. It took me two hours to get chains on the tires installed properly, hence our sunset arrival.

Because I am telling this story, it is evident we eventually arrived, all digits intact.

The next day, I load our supplies onto the red sled to transport from the car what we thought we'd need for two days back to our warm little house, woodstove blazing merrily, dogs leaping and nipping and playing.

Then, the blizzard commences in earnest.

Five days later, after draining the water heater ~ our plumbing is naturally out of commission due to frozen, broken pipes ~ we are just about out of fresh water, reduced to melting snow for washing dishes and bodies. Our lessons in the technology of evaporation teach us that a Dutch oven heaped with snow, say 6-8 inches' worth, reduces to a mere inch of water, necessitating multiple trips into the blasting wind for more.

We preserve energy with candles and flashlights, use the Remington Noiseless manual typewriter instead of the laptop, expecting the solar power to fail after days without sun, cutting us off from all communication, when I am no longer able to charge the cell phone.

What we do: Monopoly (Junior and regular), Timber, Double Solitaire, Spit, re-read the first of the Harry Potter series, listen to Ian McKellen recite Homer's *Odyssey*, manage to sled when the wind isn't too cruel, watch multiple episodes of "The Magic Schoolbus," my son creating outrageously complex Lego structures (a Batcave for the Batmobile, among others) while I read and work on my novel, hook rugs, caulk cracks, photograph frost flowers on the window, feed the fire, and worry about getting poisoned by propane fumes (the gas feeds our heater, fridge, and stove), and/or burned by unwatched candles (recalling Dickens' Miss Havisham) and becoming claustrophobic from cabin fever. But boredom never sets in: I finish my revisions, my son builds ever new and startling architectural wonders, and a week in Paradise slips by.

SAYING FAREWELL TO JONESTOWN
2010

I no longer hear Jim Jones in my ears, no longer listen to the Peoples Temple Choir belt "He's Able" as I hike the hills, no longer catalogue my cassettes of Temple voices, no longer dog-ear my books with titles like *Peoples Temple, Peoples Tomb*. After six years, three of those years with a finished novel, *Paradise Undone*, failing to enter the kingdom of print ~ yet ~ I have finally moved on to new work. Not without regret.

Marceline, Watts, Truth and Virgil, the four protagonists of P.U., or "pee-yew!" in my affectionate abbreviation, don't live in my dreams, or make me laugh with their jokes. I don't get angry at their stubbornness or want to shake them for their inability to change. The agent who believed in the book gave up after 40 rejections. I send the novel to contests: a semi-finalist last month, a finalist the month before. At least some reader saw merit, somewhere.

My new research brings me volumes from far-flung bookstores, like *The Muses Flee Hitler* and *The Refugee Intellectual*, yet when I went to my Jonestown shelves to sell no-longer-needed materials to finance the new BookSearch.com purchases, I found it hard to part with *Jesus and Jim Jones* and *Dear People: Remembering Jonestown*. I am unwilling to send my hard-to-get copies of *Journey to Nowhere* and *Hearing the Voices of Jonestown* out into the cyberworld of used book sales. Will I ever read *Let Our Children Go* or *Strategies for Survival: The Psychology of Cultural Resilience in Ethnic Minorities*? Most probably not, but my bookshelves tell their own stories, narrate my history, with or without publication of the fruits of my work.

Recently, I re-connected with a very old friend, or, more accurately, a sister of an old friend. Both sisters had been involved in a "community" for over 25 years, shunning their parents and people from their former lives, including me. My friend died during that time, apparently of natural causes, and a short while later her sister fled the group, leaving behind her child and the child of her sister. She now says, "I didn't even know I was in a *cult*."

That word choice prompts varied responses, especially when used in light of Peoples Temple. (I made sure not to use that word when speaking to her about her experience.) She read *Paradise Undone: A Novel of Jonestown* and later wrote me that it spoke to her of the huge chunk of her life spent with many wonderful people in the "community." The leader was the problem, she said, echoing the Jonestown member who said, "The only problem with Jonestown was Jones." Like Jones, the leader of this group brooked no resistance. My friend had begun to question, according to her sister, just before her death, whose circumstances remain murky.

One day, perhaps, if *Paradise Undone* is a judge's first choice at one of these book contests and finally gets published, I hope it will speak to others, to the survivors of Jonestown as well as to those who have experienced "communities" like my new/old friend, people still mulling over what happened and why, unsure if "cult" describes their experiences.

WHAT THEY CALL HIM
2014

They call him "Hot Chocolate," my mixed-race son whom everyone assumes is adopted. Unlike Barack Obama, for example, Elijah does not look biracial; the crowd assumes he plays basketball ~ and very well at that ~ due to his African-American heritage; he never disappoints. In the 99% white Christian middle school from which he has just graduated, he was the fastest runner, highest scoring shooter, most charismatic boy there.

Lest you assume this is proud mother braggadocio, be assured I came up in the world of newsprint and chain-smoking reporters: just the facts, Ma'am. I received so many compliments on his achievements throughout the years, his leadership of the 8th grade team to an undefeated season. "White Men Can't Jump," an older basketball movie that epitomized a certain haughtiness, offered a handy vocabulary for Elijah's ego-boosting.

My son has no African-American background, however. His father is French, of Haitian, Congolese, Moroccan, and Cambodian descent. On my side, he is Jewish ~ Eastern and Western European all the way back ~ including a Holocaust survivor. My German-Jewish father fled to Shanghai in 1939, then left Mao's Red Chinese government in 1949 for the United States. This pointedly detailed biography pinpoints the lack of any genetic basketball forebears whatsoever.

Elijah's skill is all his own, his drive ~ the same. His absent father did not play sports, not even soccer in Marseilles, due to childhood asthma. From me, Elijah inherited intellect and good humor, but zero by way of athletics. My physical activity focused on ballet, then jazz, then Afro-Haitian dance classes in college, though I was never very good at any of it. A worker, a "tiller in the field," as one teacher labeled me by way of compliment, but not a gifted dancer. A chubby girl, I was the proverbial last-picked for kickball in elementary school, and team sports, as in junior or high school, never even crossed my teenage radar. I did not know what "varsity" meant until my son began his life as an athlete.

This trajectory into the world of highly competitive basketball has educated me in every possible way, predictable as well as unimaginable. I never attended a sports event of any kind until Elijah wanted to see the high school boys play our 2A football season opener a few years back. Born in New York City in 1960, a girl nurtured on "Hair," Woodstock and "Fiddler on the Roof," I never realized how much of America's energy, money and time is invested in the various ways balls can enter baskets and goals, fly over nets, and slide across ice or fields in the form of pucks. Though I formerly saw myself as a sophisticated New Yorker, I now know how very little I knew.

Where was I, these 50 years and more, that I failed to recognize the greatest obsession of the American public? Overseas, you might ask? Mining ore underground? No. I resided in Academia for much of my adult life, where the crowd I hung with ~ English Department-types, primarily ~ did not talk about buzzer beaters, ally-oops, double-triples, or like vocabulary.

Hot Chocolate liked his nickname, though it made me uneasy. As we have just moved to a more cosmopolitan world, where he won't be the only person of color in school, nor the only Jew, this queasiness on my part might abate.

Our Judaism is cultural, ethical, historical, and, I like to add, culinary. Never much for synagogue, I practice our faith in my idiosyncratic way.

Fulfilling stereotypes makes me uncomfortable. As a New York Jew who's spent her adult life in very Gentile parts of the West, I know what it means when strangers make assumptions about me based on my religion, my birthplace, my nose. People see my olive skin, my generous proboscis, and assume they know me. Likewise, they observe my son ~ his long strong legs, his afro, his easy grace ~ and say, Basketball Player.

They don't say Orthodontist, Research Scientist, Financial Analyst or any other career that might accurately predict the outcome of his decidedly scientific and mathematical bent in the classroom ~ again so unlike my own proclivities. Why does this bother me?

At night, Elijah watches videos on YouTube of young brown boys actively scouted by basketball professionals. Not just high schoolers, but some in middle school, and lately, even elementary. The wunderkinds on the court are always dark-skinned, though not every boy is from the traditional inner-city background, nor the product of a single mother, like Elijah.

I don't exactly belong in that group of single-mothers-of-Black-basketball-prodigies and would never be likened to women like Le Bron James's mother, Gloria, who was 16 when she bore her son, a child who would defy every statistic of the demographic category into which he was born.

Elijah's demography is faculty brat, only ~ and spoiled ~ child, the youngest of his wealthy Jewish grandparents' progeny, a boy with a prodigious college fund awaiting post-secondary and post-graduate education, a direction all in my family expect him to take.

All invisible to the fan in the stands.

But will he follow his future there? At 14, of course he doesn't yet know for sure. At his first practice, the new coach matched him with the older brown boy on the JV for defense. I wondered about this: why, with only two brown boys in the combined JV and C teams with 22 kids all together, does a young white man with an Irish surname match Elijah with a boy I'll call Jaden? Are they the best two players there? Or does he assume the boys will be comfortable together because they share a similar complexion? Alternatively, could he be shielding the other boys, mostly white but also Chinese, Indian-from-India, and a few of mixed race (a category in which Elijah officially belongs but is never recognized as such due to his appearance) from being guarded by a zealous black boy?

Attributing such blinkered race consciousness to a young white coach in the second decade of the 21st century may sound paranoid on my part, but, as the daughter of a man who fled for his life from his native country solely because he was born a Jew, I judge others with extreme caution; they must prove themselves worthy of my trust. Worthy of entrusting my sole child to their care.

My father, 5 feet tall and fragile by the end of his 87th year, divided human beings into "he who works with his head and he who works with his hands" ~ the latter category clearly inferior to the former. The latter were necessary, of course; they changed the thinkers' tires and fixed their fridges and made life function smoothly for the brainy. The handymen were to be respected and well-paid, but not admired. Not aspired to. He never opined specifically on professional athletes, though he did adore Jack Nicklaus. If Heinz were still alive, would he be disappointed in his youngest grandson, whose existence so thrilled him?

"A grandfather at 86!" he crowed. He celebrated my child's mixed-race status prior to Elijah's birth.

A young man in Tientsin during the 1940s, Heinz had fallen in love with a Chinese woman, but both concluded it out of the question to marry, as each wanted children, and in that time and place, children of mixed race suffered, looked down upon by both groups, who saw in the mélange evidence of traitorous behavior on the part of each parent. Eventually Heinz came to America, where a child like Elijah was not only possible, but, on the cusp of the new millennium, fifty years later, longed for. Beloved.

My mother died ten years after Heinz, and she, too, bequeathed a college fund for my son. Elijah need not worry about affording the university of his choice. Yet adults said to me, while Elijah was still a toddler, "He'll be able to get an affirmative action scholarship!" Some who offered that prediction were other college professors. Those white colleagues didn't utter the phrase meanly, yet there was something insidious underlying their expression: envy! Were I to have that conversation today, I would suggest that the way the Supreme Court is going, affirmative action will be dead by 2018, when Elijah applies to school. As is by now obvious, the survival of affirmative action is irrelevant to his choice of college.

However, basketball scholarships are what he wants; this way he can stand with the other brown boys, ravenous for recognition, eager to earn it. The more I learn about basketball, the more complex it seems; the 32-page book of plays he is required to memorize before his first game, complete with notations and abbreviations on the margins, seem to me similar to sheet music, a language I never learned, unable to master the time signature or play an instrument. Elijah possesses that gift too and might have mastered his horn had he chosen music, but he scorns band, labels it "girly," in favor of sports. One doesn't become a man by playing brass; one acquires manliness on the court.

In his new world of multi-hued teammates and competition, he can't be Hot Chocolate anymore. The other teams often have boys darker chocolate than he, offering the obvious lesson of context. He's not the best anymore either – not the most talented, best looking, most able, most dedicated. On the opposing teams are hungry boys, for whom the basketball scholarship is the proverbial ticket out of poverty, a chance for mothers like Gloria James to prosper. Le Bron's story is not Elijah's story.

But it is that story nevertheless strangers conjure when they observe him playing. Nowadays, Elijah can no longer say "white men can't jump," because he plays with and against white boys who can and do. He can no longer be the guy to save the day for his team, game after game.

Today, he said he was glad to be relieved of that burden. "Everyone plays so hard here, Mom." This afternoon, his team gained their first victory and suffered their first defeat, pre-season. In the huge city gym, parents black and white and of all intermediate shades and hues commingled, their common focus the every-colored boys on the paint, vying for the ball.

Whatever stereotype audience members might attach to various players, the boys themselves, for their precious seconds on the boards, remain oblivious. As the ball soars across court, seeking the net in the slivered breath before the buzzer, I observe Elijah gazing at the precipice of hope, his last throw his only thought, his most vital self.

ESPRESSO INDUCES
1999

At Burgerville, I ordered a coffee milkshake from the car. Hugely pregnant, sweating buckets, I decided this one time only to use the drive-through, though it violated all my environmental principles. In the passenger seat, Baba, my chosen mother-figure, offered no objection.

"That comes with two shots of espresso," recited the nasal voice through the loudspeaker.

For almost 9 months, I have survived without caffeine. Determined to bring my baby into the world chemical-free, I eliminated the vice I still loved to entertain. I was 39, too old for illegal substances. Today, overwhelmed by the bright sunny world after weeks in the dark, avoiding human interaction, I decided affirmatively.

"That's fine. No whipped cream."

An hour later, we arrived at BABIES R US, a store I had sworn to avoid.

"There are no bassinets anywhere," Baba said. "Get over yourself. Could be our means to an end."

Baba and her husband, Steve, tended to me in my worst days of pre-partum depression. Nearly a month before the baby was due, I was planning to give it up for adoption, convinced I could not conquer my genetic legacy ~ generations of depressives ~ to be a "good enough" mother to Helen/Elijah. I went back on meds.

Sipping the chocolate ice cream doused in icy dark coffee through a giant straw, I felt suddenly, unreasonably high.

"All right. But we won't find anything I like. I'm sure they only have plastic."

For my baby, I refused the idea of a crib, which I equated with prison, complete with bars. I would breastfeed on demand, both of us sleeping on the mattress on the floor: no danger of him/her falling off. The baby's father slept with another woman early in the pregnancy, so I sent him away. He did not try to return.

171

Inside the cavernous store, air conditioning froze the sweat streaming from my pores, causing me to shake involuntarily, teeth chattering.

Directed to the rear of the big box, I spotted it right away. Wicker, not white but natural, on a sturdy wheeled cart. The bassinette was hooded so the baby's face could be shielded from the sun. No plastic anywhere.

Inspired by caffeine, I could not sleep that night. Literally. I tossed in my bed, hot and wide awake in the summertime humidity. In the morning, I went into labor, three weeks early. Ultimately, I would keep my baby and the bassinette, in case I decided to have another child.

That day before I gave birth, the parking lot to the Babies R Us spread acres and acres to the sun-baked horizon. I could feel the searing concrete through the thin bottoms of my flip-flops. Surely this is one version of hell, I said to Baba, giggling as if I were a teenager, stoned for the first time.

Baba, whom I trusted, a mother to three and grandmother to five, replied, "Hell sometimes disguises paradise."

STUDY GUIDE

for Readers, Discussion Groups, Teachers, and Students

These questions serve as a guide to help readers make their way through this collection of essays and deepen their understanding of this book and Annie Dawid's journey through this book. Readers can use them as ways to open discussions with others about the book. There are no right or wrong answers to these questions. Simply use them as another part of the story.

1. The title to *Put Off My Sackcloth* includes the word "Essay." Yet, in the preface, the editor likens this collection to a mosaic. Given the definition of a mosaic, what implications does the word have for the organization of *Put Off My Sackcloth* that "essay collection" may not? What other connotations does the word "mosaic" have that might apply to these essays?

2. Dawid very specifically calls attention to the dates pinpointing the year of her life the essay describes. The earliest essay covers 1976 and the most recent essay 2020. Given that these essays cover so much of Dawid's life, why do you think she chose not to put them in chronological order? What effect does the date for each essay have on your reading of the collection?

3. The essays in *Put Off My Sackcloth* are not directly spiritual essays, yet the book, including its title, contains quotes and epigraphs from the Psalms. What do you think was Dawid's purpose in creating that connection to the spiritual? How is your reading of the essays shaped by this connection?

4. Dawid refers to T.S. Eliot's famous poem, "Four Quartets," several times in the book. In her essay, "A Writer's Journal, Part II," she says that she studied the "Four Quartets" for "a kind of answer," as she dealt with her despair of the world. Given the excerpts included in the book on pages 20, 21 and 133, what kind of "answer" do you think she found in them? Or hoped to find?

5. The "spine" of the collection includes many essays describing her experience writing a novel about the Jonestown Massacre in 1978, when followers of a cult committed mass suicide at the direction of their leader.

175

Dawid becomes fixated on writing about Jonestown, giving up writing another novel she had originally planned to research, quitting her teaching job at Lewis & Clark College so she can move to the remote mountain valley of Westcliffe and continue to work on her Jonestown novel, then spending more than a decade pursuing a suitable publisher for it. Thinking about the personal stories in the other essays, why do you think the Jonestown massacre and the novel she wrote about it are so important to Dawid? How does moving back and forth between Dawid's personal stories and the Jonestown essays affect the way you read and understand this collection? What do you see as Dawid's vision for this organization?

6. Place is very important to Dawid. Why do you think this academic, cosmopolitan New York daughter of a wealthy Jewish refugee finds the remote, rural area of Westcliffe and its valley so important to her sense of well-being? As Dawid writes about Westcliffe and the inhabitants of this small community, how does she keep these essays from feeling too isolated and insular for her readers?

7. In this collection, Dawid describes several disturbing moments of crisis when she contemplates killing not only herself, but her child. How does she manage to present herself as a sympathetic narrator in these essays, one with whom the reader can empathize? Or does she? Why or why not?

8. Dawid ends her collection with an essay written about 1999, in which she is searching for a bassinet for her unborn child. The last line of the essay, the last line of the book, is spoken by Baba, a trusted wise woman, who throughout the book aids Dawid in her darkest times. Baba says, "Hell sometimes disguises paradise." Why do you think Dawid chose to end this collection with that sentence? Which moments of paradise were disguised as hell?

9. Dawid's Jewish background and the exotic lineage of her son, Elijah, are threads she returns to several times in this collection. Do the heritages of Dawid and her son serve as lenses through which Dawid sees the world? How?

10. Many publishers are hesitant about publishing essay collections instead of memoirs, convinced that readers want to read a whole "story," with a beginning, middle, and end. Many essayists choose to write what's called

"linked" essays that create an arc for the reader and the author, a feeling that the author has unveiled for the reader a journey the author takes that leads to some kind of change, some kind of transformation for the author. Do these essays chart such a journey? How would you describe this arc?

ACKNOWLEDGMENTS

Special thanks to Lindsay Lewan and Mary Tostanoski for making this book such a beautiful piece of art to hold in one's hand. Thanks to Steve and Bob for believing in Kathy's recommendation, and to Kathy: I am honored to be in your good books for essay writing, as you are such a beautiful essayist, whom I have admired for decades.

I want to acknowledge the group of students from the late 1980s at the University of Denver's English Department, Creative Writing Graduate Program, with whom I formed lifelong bonds ~ Kathy and Carol, Karen, Reg, Paul, Marck, Barb, Elizabeth, Ken (may his spirit reign with humor wherever he is) ~ who have nurtured my life as a writer from those early years to now, and, I hope, into the future. I hope I have been as a good a friend, sister writer, critic, fellow traveler to all of you as you have been to me.

And to Sally, collaborating since fifth grade.

Made in the USA
Middletown, DE
06 June 2021